Assessment &
Analytics
Guide

Printed in the U.S.A.
ISBN   978-0-545-89017-5
12 13 14 15   1838   25 24 23 22 21

4510007431

Table of Contents

Table of Contents *(continued)*

Using the *Assessment & Analytics Guide*

This guide provides teachers and leaders with an overview of the assessment and data analytic reporting components in *READ 180*.

This guide will help you:

- Screen appropriate students into *READ 180*
- Place students at an individualized point of entry into the Student Application
- Assess students throughout the year using screening, progress monitoring, curriculum-embedded, and summative measures
- Monitor reading progress for students, classes, schools, and districts
- Use data to drive instruction and group students according to their specific skill needs
- Understand a coherent approach to assessment

Contents at a Glance

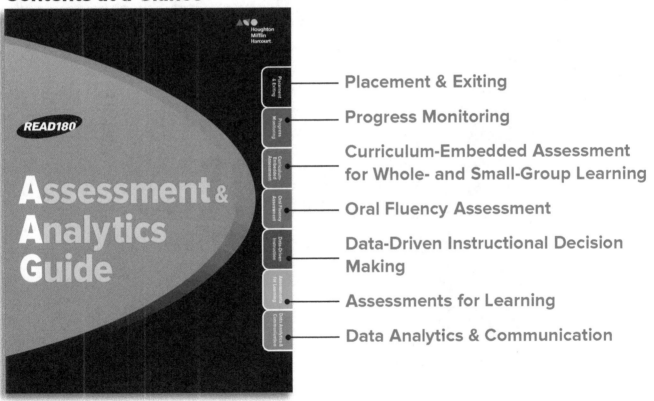

- Placement & Exiting
- Progress Monitoring
- Curriculum-Embedded Assessment for Whole- and Small-Group Learning
- Oral Fluency Assessment
- Data-Driven Instructional Decision Making
- Assessments for Learning
- Data Analytics & Communication

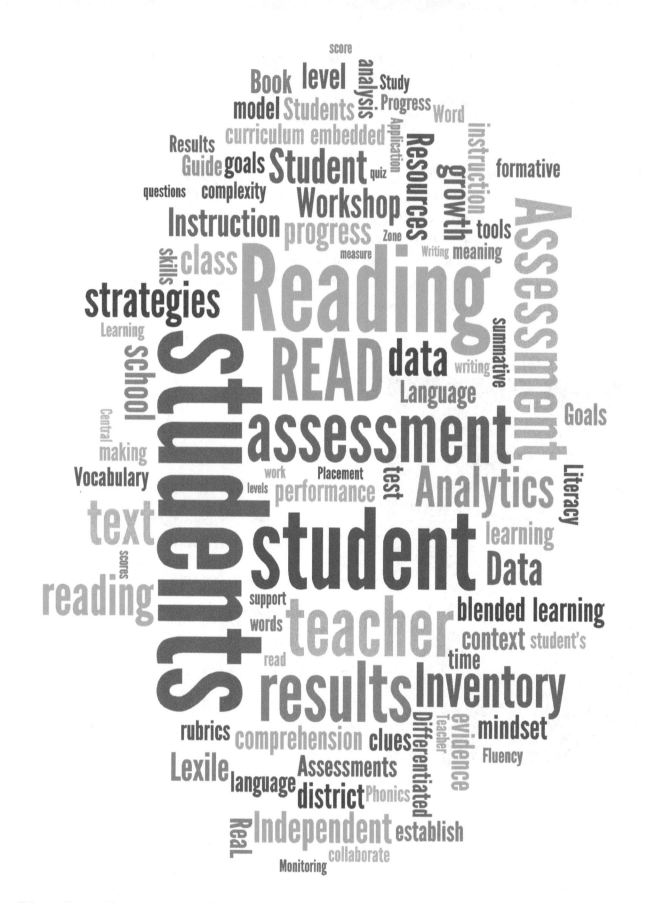

This wordle provides an at-a-glance view of the *READ 180* assessment and data analytics landscape.

Introduction:
READ 180 Universal Assessments

Comprehensive Assessment

Assessment is an essential part of the teaching and learning process.
Effective assessment provides detailed feedback on performance that can
inform instruction and enable teachers to target students' individual needs.

Assessments That Inform Instruction

1. **Screening and Placement Assessments**
   Ensure that students are appropriately targeted for intervention and receive baseline
   results that can be used to track student reading progress throughout the year.

2. **Curriculum-Embedded Assessments**
   Use as a daily instructional component to maximize student engagement while
   collecting actionable data that can be used to monitor student progress and inform
   instructional pacing.

3. **Progress Monitoring Assessments**
   Administer at regular intervals to provide updates on student performance
   and facilitate targeting of instructional support.

4. **Summative Assessments**
   Gauge student mastery of reading, writing, and listening skills through periodic
   and comprehensive assessments.

Feedback for Students and Families

Data from each assessment type is presented in reports to share with students and
their caregivers. This feedback helps students build confidence and self-esteem,
and enables families to partner in the learning process.

Informative Data for Leaders

Assessment results enable school
and district leadership to track
performance and assess implementation
effectiveness within a school or district.

*"Well-designed blended
learning solutions offer
many positive benefits for
our struggling students and
allow teachers to do what
they do best: teach with
confidence and purpose."*

Dr. Ted Hasselbring
Adaptive Technology
Professor of Special Education at Peabody
College of Vanderbilt University

READ 180/System 44 Assessment Timeline

Use this timeline to plan when to administer *READ 180* assessments throughout the course of a school year. Students in *System 44* follow a slightly different path to address foundational reading skills.*

Beginning of the Year

	Assessment	Purpose	Workshop 1
Reading Inventory™	HMH *Reading Inventory*	Screening, Placement, and Progress Monitoring	★
Phonics Inventory™	HMH *Phonics Inventory*	Screening, Placement, and Progress Monitoring	★
	Reading Counts! Quizzes	Progress Monitoring	TAKE AS NEEDED ·········
	Oral Fluency Assessments	Progress Monitoring	★
	Portfolio Assessment	Formative Assessment	DAILY ——
READ180	*READ 180* Student Application	Formative Assessment and Progress Monitoring	DAILY ——
	READ 180 ReaL Book Do Nows	Formative Assessment	DAILY ——
	READ 180 ReaL Book Formative Assessments	Formative Assessment	DAILY ——
	READ 180 Workshop Assessments: Interim	Curriculum-Embedded and Progress-Monitoring Assessment	★
	READ 180 Workshop Assessments: End of Workshop	Curriculum-Embedded and Progress-Monitoring Assessment	★
	READ 180 ReaL Book Performance Tasks	Curriculum-Embedded and Summative Assessment	
SYSTEM 44	*System 44* Student Application (including Fast Tracks)	Formative Assessment and Progress Monitoring	DAILY
	System 44 Progress-Monitoring Assessments	Progress Monitoring	★
	System 44 Summative Assessments	Summative Assessment	

*See Appendix 1 on page 188.

		Middle of the Year		End of the Year	
	Workshop 2	Workshop 3	Workshop 4	Workshop 5	Workshop 6
		★			★
		★			★
	·····································►				
			★		★
	─────────────────────────────►				
	─────────────────────────────►				
	─────────────────────────────►				
	─────────────────────────────►				
	★	★	★	★	★
	★	★	★	★	★
		★			★
	★	★	★	★	
		★			★

Assessment Cycles

READ 180 and System 44 include a variety of assessments designed to inform instruction, monitor progress, and provide continuous diagnosis.

	Assessment	Purpose	What Is Assessed	
Reading Inventory™	**HMH *Reading Inventory***	**Screening and Placement** • Screen students for appropriate intervention • Place and exit students	• Baseline reading comprehension level • Placement within READ 180	
		Progress Monitoring • Monitor student reading progress	• Current reading level • Reading gains	
Phonics Inventory™	**HMH *Phonics Inventory***	**Screening and Placement** • Screen students for appropriate intervention • Place students appropriately	• Baseline decoding and sight word reading fluency	
		Progress Monitoring • Monitor decoding and sight word reading progress	• Letter names • Sight words • Nonsense words	
READ180®	***Reading Counts!* Quizzes**	• Assess reading comprehension • Track independent reading progress	• Reading comprehension	
	Oral Fluency Assessments	• Monitor decoding and oral fluency progress	• Word recognition • Decoding speed and accuracy • Oral expressiveness	
	Portfolio Assessment	• Assess student progress and achievements	• Comprehension • Vocabulary • Writing • Speaking & listening • Independent reading progress	
	***READ 180* Student Application**	• Monitor student progress • Diagnose reading strengths and challenges • Group students for targeted instruction	• Comprehension • Vocabulary • Fluency • Phonics/Word Recognition • Spelling/Encoding • Writing	
	***READ 180* ReaL Book Do Nows**	• Monitor retention of vocabulary acquisition	• High-utility academic words and domain-specific vocabulary • Use of specific grammar targets • Comprehension strategies	

When	Results	Informing Instruction
Three times a year	**Screening and Placement** Normative Data NCE, Stanine, Percentile Performance Standards Below Basic, Basic, Proficient, Advanced	**IF students are reading at grade level...** ...use grade-level curriculum. **IF students are reading far below grade level...** ...administer *Phonics Inventory*.
	Progress Monitoring Same as above.	**USE results to...** ...track student reading growth. ...assign appropriate instructional and independent reading materials.
Three times a year	**Screening and Placement** Percent accurate and fluent in Letter Names, Sight Words, and Nonsense Words	**IF student is a Pre- or Beginning Decoder:** ...enroll in *System 44*, Series 1. **IF student is a Developing Decoder:** ...enroll in *System 44*, Series 4. **IF student is an Advancing Decoder:** ...enroll in *READ 180*.
	Progress Monitoring *Phonics Inventory* fluency scores *Phonics Inventory* decoding status	**IF a student's *Phonics Inventory* fluency score is not improving:** ...review student-level reports data to adjust teacher-led instruction and provide additional practice.
When students complete books and eReads in Independent Reading	**Quizzes Passed** Number of quizzes attempted Percentage of goal achieved Motivation to stretch (Challenge quizzes)	**IF students are not meeting individual goals...** ...provide additional support in daily independent reading.
Three times a year	**Oral Fluency Results** Percentile based on WCPM (words correct per minute)	**IF students need further support...** ...provide phonics support from the *Foundational Reading Guide* or fluency support from Resources for Differentiated Instruction at *ReaL Book* Checkpoints.
Daily	**Writing Rubric Results** Results align to writing type assessed **Workshop Rubric Results** Progress and performance on *ReaL Book* tasks, including projects	**USE writing rubric results to...** ...provide support in revision during each End-of-Workshop Checkpoint. **USE Workshop rubric results to...** ...monitor overall performance and share results.
Daily	**Comprehension Strategies** Description, Sequence, Cause and Effect, Problem and Solution, Compare and Contrast, Central Idea and Details, Summary, Making Inferences, Author's Purpose, Point of View, Context Clues **Other Results** Phonics, spelling, fluency, writing	**IF students need further support...** ...regroup students to provide targeted support during small-group rotations. ...monitor Student App usage. **IF students need a challenge...** ...provide opportunities to apply skills with less scaffolding or Extend lessons. ...ensure appropriate level on the technology.
Daily	Correctly demonstrate use of high-utility academic vocabulary words in context.	**USE Do Now results to...** ...provide immediate oral feedback to students about grammar, vocabulary, and strategies.

Assessment Cycles *(continued)*

	Assessment	Purpose	What Is Assessed	
READ180	**READ 180 ReaL Book** Formative Assessments	• Monitor student's mastery of the Whole- and Small-Group Lesson goals • Adapt instruction	• Literacy and Language goals	
	READ 180 Workshop Assessments: Interim	• Measure acquisition of *ReaL Book* Workshop strategies • Group students for additional support • Adapt instruction	• Comprehension • Vocabulary/Word Study	
	READ 180 Workshop Assessments: End of Workshop	• Measure acquisition of *ReaL Book* Workshop strategies • Group students for additional support • Adapt instruction	• Comprehension • Vocabulary/Word Study • Critical reading • Transitions • Conventions; Writing	
	READ 180 ReaL Book Performance Tasks	• Measure acquisition of *ReaL Book* Workshop strategies	• Comprehension • Vocabulary/Word Study • Integrating information from multiple sources • Writing; Research • Listening and speaking skills	
SYSTEM 44	**System 44** Student Application (including Fast Tracks)	• Monitor student progress • Diagnose reading strengths and challenges • Group students for targeted instruction	• Decoding Accuracy • Decoding Fluency • Spelling • Comprehension • Oral Reading Fluency	
		Fast Tracks • Data-driven, adaptive placement to accelerate the pace of learning	• Decoding • Morphology • Word-Level Fluency	
	System 44 Progress-Monitoring Assessments	• Monitor student progress	• Phonemic Awareness and Phonics • Sight Words and Spelling • Morphology	
	System 44 Summative Assessments	• Evaluate transfer of newly acquired skills	• Phonemic Awareness and Phonics • Sight Words and Spelling • Morphology	

When	Results	Informing Instruction
Daily Twice per Whole- and Small- Group Lesson	Demonstrate understanding of Literacy and Language goals	**USE results to...** ...make instructional adjustments.
Once per workshop (Optional: at the end of Part 1)	**Test results** Comprehension, Vocabulary/ Word Study	**IF students need further support/challenge...** ...review *READ 180* Reports to cross-reference results. ...regroup students and provide targeted support during Small-Group rotations and at Checkpoints.
Once per workshop (At the end of Part 2)	**Test Results** Comprehension, Vocabulary/Word Study, Transitions, Conventions, Constructed Response: Critical Thinking, Writing Prompt	**IF students need further support/challenge...** ...review student test results and explain errors. ...regroup students and provide targeted support during Small-Group rotations and at Checkpoints.
Midyear; **End of Year**	**Writing Rubric Results** Results align to Research Rubric	**USE writing and presentation rubric results to...** ...provide feedback on effective research techniques, correctly citing sources, and using results to create an engaging and effective presentation.
Daily Occurs automatically for appropriate students before a new Series on the software (approximately every one–two weeks)	**Progress Monitoring** **Reading Progress** Current progress Software usage Cumulative performance	**IF a student has a median session time of less than 15 minutes...** ...ensure student gets adequate time on the Student App. **IF a student's software scores are below 70 percent...** ...provide remediation in areas of skill need during Checkpoints.
	Fast-Tracks Number of topics Fast-Tracked Individual student's RTI Median RTI	**IF a student Fast-Tracked 10 or more topics:** ...*System 44* Student App is meeting the needs of students who have already mastered certain skills. ...student's RTI will likely be above the median RTI. **IF a student's progress and mastery is consistently below the median RTI:** ...review student-level reports data to adjust teacher-led instruction and provide additional practice. ...determine if student Fast-Tracked any topics.
Five times per year	*System 44* **Progress Monitoring Assessment:** **Answer Key & Score Sheet** Number of items correct for each part and for the entire test	**IF a student does not pass a Progress Monitoring Test:** ...consider review and reteaching for skills not maintained over time. ...regroup for teacher-led instruction.
Midyear; **End of Year**	*System 44* **Midyear and End-of-Year Assessment: Answer Key & Score Sheet** Number of items correct for each part and for the entire test	**IF a student does not pass a Summative Assessment:** ...consider review and reteaching for skills not maintained over time. ...regroup for teacher-led instruction.

Understanding HMH Teacher Central

READ 180 Universal provides teachers with everything they need to facilitate effective instruction for Whole-and Small-Group Learning. HMH Teacher Central is a learning management system that empowers educators with the tools they need to maximize their instructional impact providing actionable data, instructional planning, enhanced assessment and observation tools, and professional learning—all from one space.

1 Data Dashboard

Teachers access student analytics and class-readiness metrics that inform daily lesson planning, while real-time progress metrics allow teachers to quickly monitor student performance and adjust instruction accordingly.

2 Student Bookshelf

Review student reading lists, class favorites, title recommendations, and text complexity metrics with a focus on engagement and growth.

3 Resources

Search through hundreds of point-of-use resources including professional learning videos, research, and additional instructional tools and activities for each Workshop.

4 Digital Teacher's Edition

Launch daily teaching and learning using the *ReaL Book* Digital Teacher's Edition.

5 Data Widgets

Access customizable data snapshots to quickly monitor student performance and fidelity of implementation.

Understanding the Data Dashboard

The Data Dashboard provides access to student analytics and class-readiness metrics that inform daily lesson planning so you can adjust instruction accordingly.

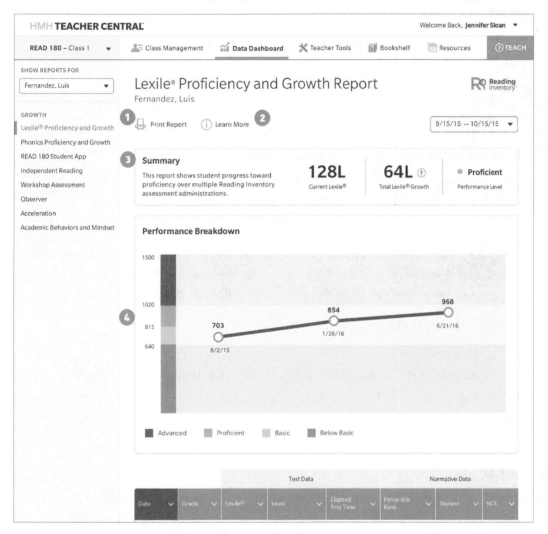

① Print Report

Select **Print** to export a printable PDF that you can save and email. You can also batch print the report for each student in the class.

② Learn More

Access **Learn More** for comprehensive information and guidance for understanding and using report data.

③ Summary

The **Summary** presents high-level takeaways based on the specific data set.

④ *Reading Inventory* Results

Monitor Lexile® proficiency and growth for placement and progress review. Encourage students to stretch their skills by selecting texts in the demanding range when they have background information about the topic or are highly motivated to read.

Understanding How to Access Resources

Use the Resources tab in HMH Teacher Central to access thousands of searchable resources, including materials for differentiation, extra practice, assessment, and professional learning videos.

Resource Collections

Resources are organized into Collections for easy identification and exploration. Resources displays several rows of collections including:

Featured Resources:

- Featured Research
- Implementation Support
- Editor's Picks
- Foundational Reading

All Workshops: Resources for each Workshop, including Instructional Routines, Resources for Differentiated Instruction, and Anchor Videos

Student Application: Anchor Video summaries and leveled passages to support the Student App

Independent Reading: Book summaries, QuickWrites, and graphic organizers to support Independent Reading

Professional Learning: Print and video resources to support professional learning

Search and Browse

While the initial Resources screen presents Collections based on the class you select, you can also use the Resources search bar to find resources of any kind. Use one of the following two search options:

- Click the arrow next to **View All Resources** at the top right of the screen. View a comprehensive list of resources. Then use the filters to narrow your search.
- Enter a resource name or keyword in the search field at the top right.

Learn More!
See pg. 179

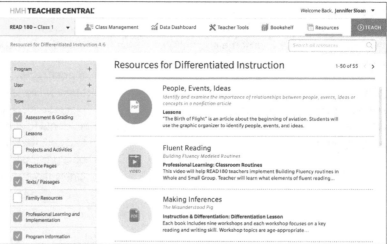

Understanding the Digital Teacher's Edition

The Digital Teacher's Edition is your primary resource for guiding Whole- and Small-Group Learning. Digital teaching tools help you optimize face-to-face instruction through multimedia displays that enhance learning and build academic engagement, point-of-use formative assessment, just-in-time data, differentiated resources, and professional development.

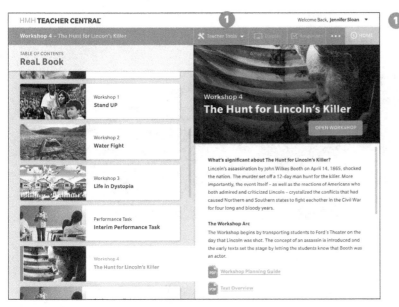

❶ Teacher Tools

Find the **Observe Board**, a digital formative assessment tool with real-time data, the **Flightboard** to show students their current group and rotation, the **Groupinator®** to organize daily *ReaL Book* instruction and Workshop Checkpoints, and the **Assignment Board** to deliver, review, and comment on student tasks.

❷ Lesson Planning

Teachers can access every lesson plan and resource they need to teach an entire Workshop effectively, allowing them to focus on what they do best: differentiating instruction and building relationships.

Understanding Teacher Tools

Easy-to-use classroom management tools enhance teaching and learning by providing everything educators need to maximize their instructional impact.

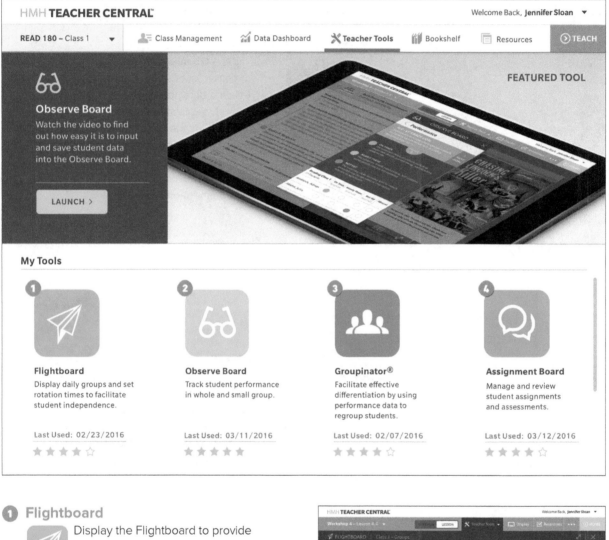

Flightboard

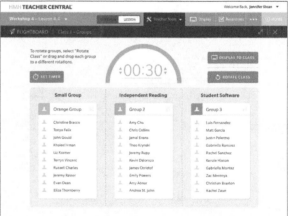

Display the Flightboard to provide guidance to students during rotations, as well as to increase student independence and class efficiency.

② The Observe Board

The Observe Board supports teachers in observing and monitoring students' progress during instruction and targeting where they need help most. Use the Observe Board to:

- Track mastery of each day's literacy and language goals
- Use rubrics aligned to each literacy and language goal to effectively and efficiently measure mastery and determine whether students are On Track, Nearly There, or Not Yet
- Record student-specific notes and send reminders to effectively differentiate instruction

③ The Groupinator

The Groupinator dynamically assigns students to groups for small-group rotations. The Groupinator provides recommended resources for each group that link directly to the Resources tab. The Groupinator allows you to:

- Choose the number of groups. Select the number of groups that matches your model for blended learning
- Group students by criteria such as: Reading Comprehension, Language and Vocabulary, Lexile measure, and Workshop Assessment data
- Rearrange instructional groups for Small-Group Learning by dragging-and-dropping student names

④ The Assignment Board

The Assignment Board enables you to assign, review, and comment on student work. Use the Assignment Board to grade:

- Workshop Assessments constructed-response items and writing prompt
- Student App Writing Zone activities
- Student App Fluency Check (Final Recording)

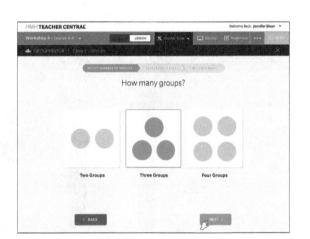

Understanding Leader Reports

Leaders can access the Data Dashboard to view reports to track program usage and reading progress for classes, teachers, grades, schools, or an entire district to ensure that students are getting the maximum benefits from *READ 180*.

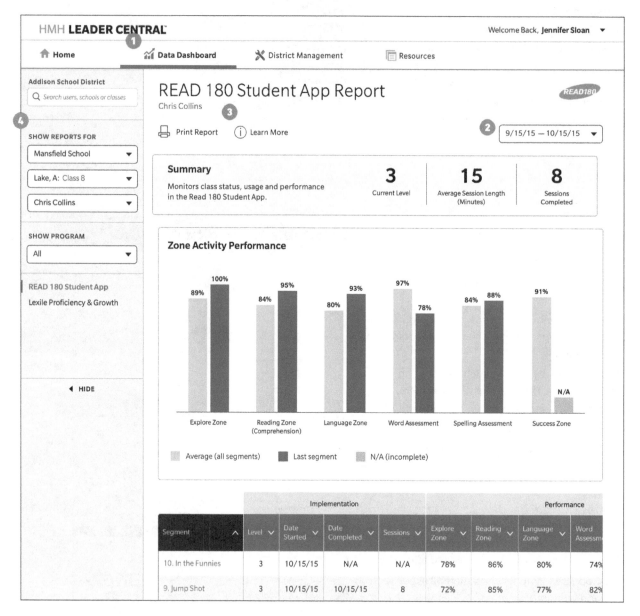

1 Data Dashboard
Access all leader reports from the **Data Dashboard**.

2 Time Period
Customize the time period to view results across the entire school year or any meaningful time period.

3 Learn More
Access **Learn More** for comprehensive information and guidance for understanding and using report data.

4 Show Reports For
Within a district, filter results for an individual school, class, or student.

Understanding Student Central

Building motivation and self-regulation, *READ 180* students can track their progress toward literacy and language skills mastery in this dynamic space.

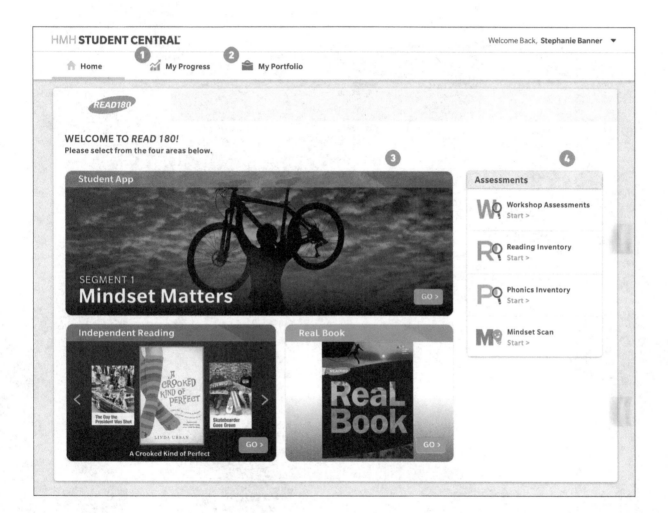

① My Progress
Students review their performance and keep track of work left to complete in each topic, segment, and zone.

② My Portfolio
Students access Workshops, graded and ungraded assignments, and teacher's comments.

③ Rotation Options
After logging into Student Central, students can access the Student App, the Independent Reading Bookshelf, or their *Real Book Workshop.*

④ Assessments
Teachers use the Assignment Board to assign as assessment; students launch the test from here.

READ180®

Assessment & Analytics Guide

Houghton
Mifflin
Harcourt

Placement
& Exiting

Curriculum-
Embedded
Assessment

Oral Fluency
Assessment

Data-Driven
Instruction

Assessment
for Learning

Data Analytics &
Communication

Placement & Exiting

This section provides background on the universal screener and placement assessments that will ensure students are properly placed into the right level of *READ 180*. It also offers criteria for when it is time for students to exit the program.

Multi-Tiered System of Supports

Utilizing a **Multi-Tiered System of Supports (MTSS)** creates a coherent continuum of evidence-based, system-wide practices that support a rapid response to the academic and behavioral needs of students. Within a MTSS, there is frequent data-based monitoring to inform instructional decision making so as to empower all students to achieve high standards (Kansas MTSS, 2008).

Response to Intervention (RTI) is a multilevel system for maximizing student achievement by integrating ongoing assessment of student progress with increasingly intensive intervention (National Center on Response to Intervention, 2010). RTI organizes intervention into multiple tiers of support for students not making adequate progress (Feldman, 2009). In all tiers of intervention, students benefit from teachers' use of data to determine whether students are making the desired academic gains, and then whether they need modifications in their curricula, materials, or instruction (Fuchs & Fuchs, 2007; Duffy, 2008).

To support students' academic, behavioral, and social needs, many schools have adopted multi-tiered models of prevention. Because Tier 3 interventions are costly in terms of time and resources, schools must find efficient and effective Tier 2 interventions prior to providing such intense supports (Bruhn, Hirsch, Gorsh, & Hannan, 2014).

Multi-Tiered System of Support Model

Tiers of Intervention

States and districts may define the RTI instructional model according to students' needs. One of the most common structures is the 3-Tier Intervention Model shown here.

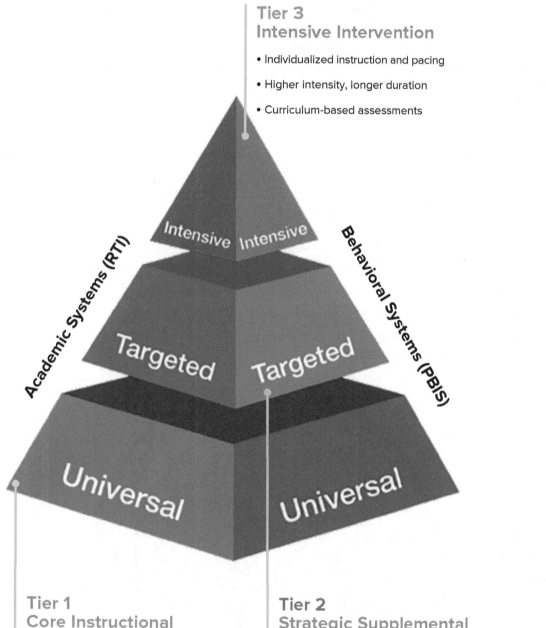

Tier 3
Intensive Intervention

- Individualized instruction and pacing
- Higher intensity, longer duration
- Curriculum-based assessments

Tier 1
Core Instructional Programs

- Differentiated support for all students
- Proactive strategies that use a variety of instructional groupings to allow optimal access to curriculum

Tier 2
Strategic Supplemental Instruction

- Supplemental curricula for students who are not successful in Tier 1
- Explicit, rapid-response, short-term instruction
- Instruction oriented toward small groups of students

Multi-Tiered System of Supports *(continued)*

Positive Behavioral Interventions and Supports (PBIS) is a system that provides supports that increase in intensity, based on students' behavioral and social needs. The purpose of PBIS is to take a proactive approach to addressing school discipline by promoting positive behaviors school-wide, identifying problem behaviors early, and responding to and reducing those behaviors through research-based instruction and intervention (Stewart, et al., 2007). At each level, key components of the model include clearly defined expectations explicitly taught to all students, opportunities for students to practice the skills, reinforcement for students who meet expectations, and a system for monitoring student progress (Lane, Robertson, & Graham-Bailey, 2006; Sugai, et al., 2000).

Schools that have a culture that includes PBIS are able to establish the behavioral supports that are needed for all children to achieve both social and academic success. These schools have demonstrated increased achievement on both academic and social measures (Cohen, Kincaid, & Childs, 2007).

Effective PBIS implementations can be found in schools and districts that:

- Foster positive social interactions between students, teachers, and administrators
- Teach behavioral expectations in a socially and age-appropriate way
- Reinforce positive behavior with methods that are targeted toward students
- Use implementation and student-level data to drive instruction and intervention (Bruhn, Hirsch, Gorsh, & Hannan, 2014)

Multi-Tiered Prevention Model

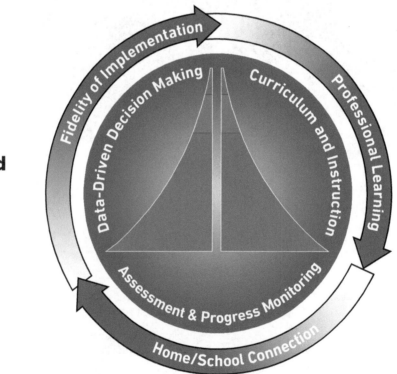

MTSS Principles in Practice

		Intervention
Tier	**Goal**	**Practice**
Tier 3	Reduce harm	• Offer interventions including mental health counseling, one-to-one tutoring, wraparound services (e.g., school, parents, community), and functional behavorial assessment-based interventions. • Support tertiary interventions that require more extensive monitoring and which are reserved for students with complex, long-term, resistant behavioral or academic issues. • Refer to a multidisciplinary team to determine if special education services are warranted.
Tier 2	Reverse harm	• Focus on more intensive strategies to respond to existing problem behaviors. • Address acquisition (can't do), fluency (trouble doing), and performance (won't do) deficits. • Respond to existing behaviors within the classroom with low-intensity strategies including: active supervision, proximity, pacing, praise, opportunities to respond, and instructive feedback. Examples include behavior contracts, self-monitoring, small-group instruction in social/behavior skills, Behavior Education Program (BEP), or Check-In/Check-Out (CICO).
Tier 1	Prevent harm from occurring	• Arrange the room to facilitate instruction. • Explicitly teach and reinforce school-wide rules/expectations. • Provide procedures and routines to facilitate smooth transitions and maximize instructional time. • Use evidence-based instructional methods. • Establish a positive classroom climate.

Multi-Tiered System of Supports (continued)

RTI in READ 180

READ 180 supports and complements an RTI model through universal screening, evidence-based intervention, and ongoing progress monitoring for data-based decision making. READ 180 engages and motivates struggling readers with age-appropriate materials at multiple reading levels. Educators can use READ 180 data to guide instruction and meet key principles of RTI.

Universal Screening With the HMH Reading Inventory

In an RTI model, screening is typically conducted three times a year. Universal screening should be brief, reliable, and valid, and should appropriately identify students who require more intense intervention to meet established benchmarks. Use The Reading Inventory to initially screen and monitor the growth of students throughout the year. The Lexile® Framework allows each student's Lexile reader measure to be aligned to performance standards that can be used for placement decisions.

Baseline Measure and Placement

Once students have completed their initial, or baseline, Reading Inventory test and are recommended for READ 180, HMH Teacher Central will use their results to place them into the appropriate READ 180 level in the Student Application. Students build reading proficiency by practicing skills using age-appropriate material at their current reading level. Elementary students with initial Lexile® measures below 400L and secondary students with initial Lexile measures below 600L should take The Phonics Inventory to determine if those students are able to identify sight words and decode nonsense words fluently. Students who have not yet mastered their foundational reading skills would likely benefit more from placement in an explicit and systematic phonics program, such as System 44. For placement recommendations, refer to charts.

Fall Placement Recommendations (Current School Year)*			
Current Grade	Eligibile for Tier 2/READ 180 or Tier 3/System 44	Eligible for READ 180	Eligible for Tier 1
4	BR to 400L	405 to 515L	520L and Above
5	BR to 400L	405 to 735L	740L and Above
6	BR to 600L	605 to 825L	830L and Above
7	BR to 600L	605 to 920L	925L and Above
8	BR to 600L	605 to 965L	970L and Above
9	BR to 600L	605 to 1005L	1010L and Above
10	BR to 600L	605 to 1045L	1050L and Above
11 and 12	BR to 600L	605 to 1075L	1080L and Above
Recommendation	Administer The Phonics Inventory to determine if READ 180/Tier 2 or System 44/Tier 3 is more appropriate.	Enroll in READ 180 or Tier 2 Intervention.	Enroll in Core program.

*Fall is from July 15–November 30 of current school year. Grade level corresponds to grade level at time of testing within fall window. See Appendix 2 on page 189.

Frequent Monitoring of Student Progress

In an RTI model, data should be regularly collected and analyzed to determine whether instruction is producing the desired academic results. *READ 180* provides continuous assessment and immediate feedback for students and teachers. HMH Teacher Central gathers and displays quantifiable student performance results in detailed reports that allow teachers to identify and measure student skill and strategy mastery.

Data-Driven Differentiation

In an RTI model, classroom instruction should be differentiated to ensure that students will achieve established benchmarks. *READ 180* includes extensive embedded support for differentiating classroom instruction to address students' needs. Each *ReaL Book* Digital Teacher's Edition lesson includes two formative assessments from which data is used to regroup students and recommend differentiated small-group lessons. Students are also placed at appropriate levels and receive individualized support during the Student Application and Independent Reading Rotations.

Spring Placement Recommendations (Current School Year)*			
Current Grade	Eligibile for Tier 2/*READ 180* or Tier 3/*System 44*	Eligible for *READ 180*	Eligible for Tier 1
4	BR to 400L	405 to 735L	740L and Above
5	BR to 400L	405 to 825L	830L and Above
6	BR to 600L	605 to 920L	925L and Above
7	BR to 600L	605 to 965L	970L and Above
8	BR to 600L	605 to 1005L	1010L and Above
9	BR to 600L	605 to 1045L	1050L and Above
10	BR to 600L	605 to 1075L	1080L and Above
11 and 12	BR to 600L	605 to 1180L	1185L and Above
Recommendation	Administer *The Phonics Inventory* to determine if *READ 180*/Tier 2 or *System 44*/Tier 3 is more appropriate.	Enroll in *READ 180* or Tier 2 Intervention.	Enroll in Core program.

*Spring is from April 1–July 14 of the current school year. Grade level corresponds to grade level at time of testing within spring window. See Appendix 3 on page 190.

Universal Screening

Universal Screening With the HMH *Phonics Inventory*

READ 180 also includes a screening measure to help identify students who will most benefit from the *System 44* individualized learning technology: *The Phonics Inventory*.

The Phonics Inventory is a computer-based test of basic letter recognition, decoding skills, and sight word knowledge. This targeted screener and progress monitor measures foundational reading skills, including the accuracy and fluency with which students identify individual letters and words and decode nonwords. *The Reading Inventory* is a screener and progress monitor that measures reading comprehension, a skill that requires sufficient fluency with foundational skills. Since students in *System 44* and similar Tier 3 interventions are still developing foundational skills, their growth is more accurately measured with *The Phonics Inventory*. Only once students are advancing decoders is *The Reading Inventory* an appropriate measure of their reading growth.

Identifying Students

Struggling readers vary in their particular strengths and challenges. It is important to screen students who may benefit more from using *System 44* to ensure that the Student Application instruction is appropriate for their specific skill needs.

Students who are candidates for *System 44* may struggle with:

- Basic phonemic awareness
- Decoding and word recognition
- Word-level fluency
- Strategies for reading unfamiliar words
- Reading text two or more years below grade level

Screening Into System 44

The flowchart below demonstrates the two primary paths for screening students into *System 44* using *The Reading Inventory* and *The Phonics Inventory*.

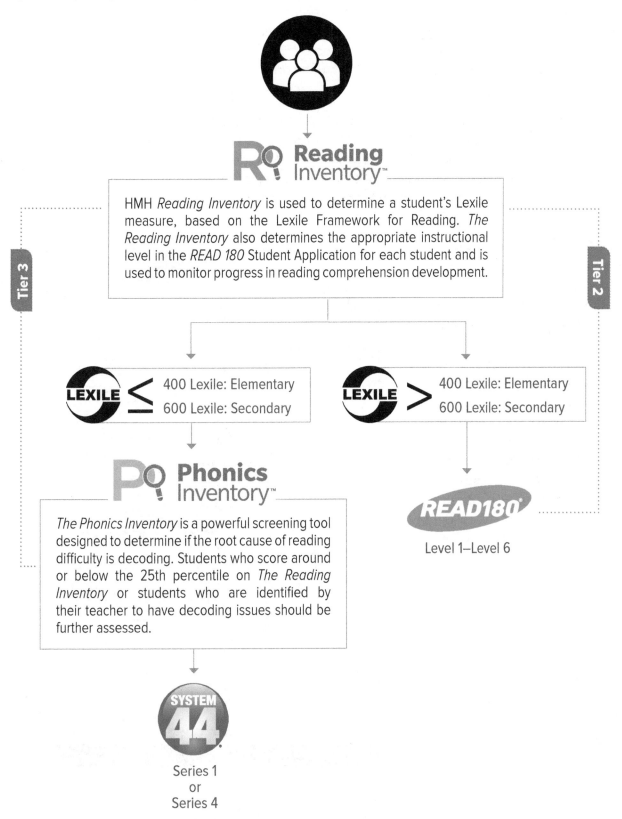

Reading Inventory™

HMH *Reading Inventory* is used to determine a student's Lexile measure, based on the Lexile Framework for Reading. *The Reading Inventory* also determines the appropriate instructional level in the *READ 180* Student Application for each student and is used to monitor progress in reading comprehension development.

Tier 3

Tier 2

LEXILE ≤ 400 Lexile: Elementary
600 Lexile: Secondary

LEXILE > 400 Lexile: Elementary
600 Lexile: Secondary

Phonics Inventory™

The Phonics Inventory is a powerful screening tool designed to determine if the root cause of reading difficulty is decoding. Students who score around or below the 25th percentile on *The Reading Inventory* or students who are identified by their teacher to have decoding issues should be further assessed.

READ180®

Level 1–Level 6

SYSTEM 44

Series 1
or
Series 4

HMH *Reading Inventory*

The HMH *Reading Inventory* is an objective, research-based assessment of students' reading comprehension ability that can be used to screen and place students. Based on the Lexile Framework for Reading, *The Reading Inventory* can be administered to any reader, regardless of age and grade level. *Reading Inventory* is a computer-adaptive test designed for quick administration in an untimed, low-pressure environment.

The Reading Inventory can be administered at the beginning of the school year to determine each student's baseline reading level. *The Reading Inventory* produces a Lexile measure, which is recorded in HMH Teacher Central. Students with Lexile measures of BR–400L (elementary) and BR–600L (secondary) may lack decoding skills and should take *The Phonics Inventory* for possible screening into *System 44*.

The Lexile Framework

The Reading Inventory is based on the Lexile Framework, which measures texts and readers on the same scale. The Lexile Framework is a reliable and tested tool designed to bridge two critical aspects of student reading achievement—leveling text difficulty and assessing the reading skills of each student. The Lexile scale ranges from Beginning Reader to above 1500L. Any score below 100L is reported as BR, or Beginning Reader. When a reader's Lexile measure matches the Lexile measure of a text, the reader experiences confidence and control over the reading process.

How *The Reading Inventory* Works

During a *Reading Inventory* test, students read brief passages from literature and nonfiction and answer questions about what they have read. Each test screen contains a passage and a question.

Computer-Adaptive Assessment

As a computer-adaptive test, *The Reading Inventory* adjusts item difficulty to students' responses. As students progress through the assessment, the difficulty levels of questions change according to students' performance. As the student correctly answers questions, the Lexile of each question increases. When the student answers a question incorrectly, the next question presented is at a lower Lexile level. The assessment stops once the student has answered a sufficient number of questions to determine an accurate Lexile measure.

Sample Student Reading Inventory Performance

The bar graph below represents a sample student's performance on one *Reading Inventory* test. Each question is numbered. Questions answered correctly are blue; incorrect answers are orange. Note how the level of test items adjusts to the student's responses. This graph is only a sample. The number of questions and the Lexile of each question depend on individual student performance.

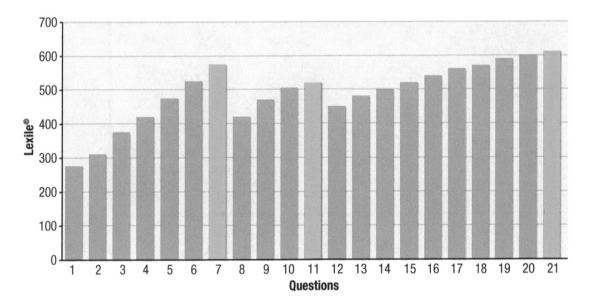

Using *The Reading Inventory* Results for Placement

Reading Inventory results help teachers establish a baseline measure, place students in the appropriate level, form groups, and differentiate instruction.

Matching Reading Level in the *READ 180* Student Application

Research has shown that readers make the most progress and develop lifelong reading enjoyment when they are given texts that match their reading level instead of reading material that is too challenging. Once students have completed their initial *Reading Inventory*, their baseline results are used to place them into an appropriate *READ 180* Student Application level. Students will use the Student Application to practice reading skills with texts at their level.

The following table lists the Lexile range for each *READ 180* level in each stage:

Student App Reading Levels

Lexile Measure	450	500	550	600	650	700	750	800	850	900	950	1000	1050	1100	1150	1200	1250	1300

Student App Levels: Level 1, Level 2, Level 3, Level 4, Level 5, Level 6

Elementary Stage A

Middle School Stage B

High School Stage C

2nd Grade Reading Level — 7th Grade Reading Level — 9th Grade Reading Level — 12th Grade Reading Level

Matching Student to Text in Independent Reading Struggling readers often need assistance in choosing appropriate books and articles to read independently. *READ 180* provides a text complexity measure for every paperback, audiobook, eReads article, and *ReaL Book* reading. Each text has been assessed by multiple reviewers who have considered three key aspects of text complexity:

1. Qualitative Measure

2. Quantitative Measure

3. Reader and Task

Consider the trajectory of text complexity as you help students select appropriate books in the Independent Reading Rotation.

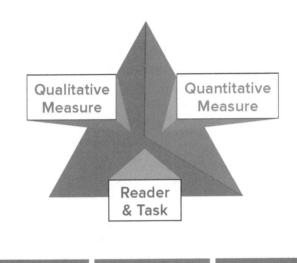

Qualitative Measures:

HMH measures the levels of meaning, structure, language, conventionality/clarity, and knowledge demands of increasingly complex texts. Students receive decreasing scaffolding in order to demonstrate growth and move toward independence.

Quantitive Measures:

The Lexile Framework measures fiction and nonfiction texts and readers on the same scale.

Reader & Task Considerations:

HMH supports teachers as they match reader to task. *READ 180* provides carefully calibrated, high-interest texts in a variety of formats to maximize student choice and engagement. Highly motivated students read more. As they read, they build content-area knowledge and gain ability and expertise as readers.

HMH *Reading Inventory* (continued)

Focusing on Quantitative Measure

The quantitative aspects of a text include its word length or frequency, difficulty of vocabulary, and sentence length. The quantitative measure of a *READ 180* text is its Lexile measure.

Quantitative
Measure

The Lexile Framework for Reading provides a common scale for matching reader ability with text complexity, allowing easy monitoring of student progress. Lexile scores allow teachers to track student progress and assign each student appropriate reading materials. For example, if a text is too difficult for readers, they may struggle, quickly become frustrated, and give up. On the other hand, if the text is too easy, readers may not be challenged and become easily distracted or bored.

Students' Lexile scores are the level at which they can read with moderate success—about 75% comprehension. Use *Reading Inventory* results to help students select books and eReads at appropriate reading levels during Independent Reading. Review the chart below to support students with their independent reading.

Text Difficulty	Lexile Range	Use This Range When
Easy/Fluent	100L–250L below student's *Reading Inventory* score	Encouraging reluctant readers.
On-Level	100L below–50L above student's *Reading Inventory* score	Assigning independent reading. Most independent reading should be completed at this level.
Challenging	50L–250L above student's *Reading Inventory* score	Students have background knowledge or are highly motivated.

While students should be encouraged to move on to more demanding texts as their skills develop and their *Reading Inventory* scores increase, it is not necessary for them to advance to a higher Lexile measure with each new book or article. By reading half a dozen titles within their "On-Level" range, students build reading comprehension before moving on to a higher level.

Focusing on Qualitative Measure

The qualitative measure of a text includes its levels of meaning, structure, language clarity, and background knowledge requirements. For example, a simple text has a clear purpose, literal language, and requires little prior knowledge. A more complex text may have an implied purpose, unconventional structure, and require the reader to have specific background information. Additional qualitative components of text complexity considered by *READ 180* Universal include those identified by Coh-Metrix as the most important factors in readability: narrativity, syntactic simplicity, word concreteness, referential cohesion, and deep cohesion (Graesser, McNamara, & Kulikowich, 2011).

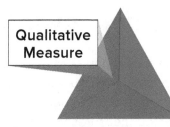

Qualitative Measure

READ 180 provides a text complexity measure for every text, including paperbacks, audiobooks, and eReads found in the Independent Reading rotation. Multiple reviewers have assessed each text and rated the text according to the following scale.

Basic   Moderate 1   Moderate 2   Complex 1   Complex 2

Texts were assigned a qualitative measure score based on the following factors:

Purpose/Levels of Meaning	
One level of meaning ⟶	Multiple levels of meaning (used for fiction texts)
Single, stated purpose ⟶	Unstated purpose; multiple purposes (used for nonfiction texts)
Text Structure	
Simple, conventional structure ⟶	Complex, unconventional structure
Chronological ⟶	Interrupted chronology
Simple graphics support text ⟶	Sophisticated graphics add essential information
Language	
Literal, clear language ⟶	Figurative, ironic, or ambiguous language
Current, familiar word choice ⟶	Archaic, unfamiliar word choice
Conversational language ⟶	Academic language
Knowledge Demands	
One simple theme ⟶	Complex, sophisticated themes
One perspective ⟶	Multiple perspectives
Familiar content or ideas ⟶	Unfamiliar content or ideas
No references to other texts ⟶	Multiple references to other texts

HMH *Reading Inventory* (continued)

Quantitative readability formulas give a rough index of the overall difficulty of the text's syntax and vocabulary demands, whereas the qualitative measure of text complexity focuses on dimensions of texts that readability formulas typically cannot capture. In combination, these measures yield an overview of how challenging a text is and in what ways.

Focusing on Reader and Task

Beyond matching students to texts of appropriate reading levels, it is also important to consider reader variables, such as level of motivation and interest, as well as the reading task assigned. Use the Bookshelf in HMH Teacher Central to help students select books on topics that interest them.

Matching Student to Text in Whole- and Small-Group Learning

In addition to placing students at appropriate levels in the Student Application and Independent Reading rotations, *Reading Inventory* results are also used to group students and differentiate instruction during Whole- and Small-Group Learning.

The Groupinator™ places students into groups based on their *Reading Inventory* results. These grouping recommendations help determine what level of scaffolding to provide during Small-Group Learning. Access Support and Extend lessons in the Digital Teacher's Edition to support students at varying reading levels.

HMH *Phonics Inventory*

The Phonics Inventory is designed to identify older struggling readers who require systematic and explicit phonics instruction to strengthen foundational skills necessary for fluency and reading comprehension.

The Phonics Inventory contains three equivalent test forms to screen and place students into *System 44* and to help monitor their progress at key points throughout the program. *The Phonics Inventory* also includes reports and resources, as well as test accommodations.

The Phonics Inventory measures both accuracy and fluency by identifying the number of correct answers as well as the speed (or latency) of student response. It identifies students who may lack decoding skills, as well as those who possess certain skills but cannot apply or transfer them effectively or quickly enough to comprehend text.

The assessment is brief (10–12 minutes) and can be administered to multiple students concurrently. It consists of four sections:

- **Practice Test** (11 items), a warm-up activity that orients students to the interface
- **Letter Recognition** (11 items), assessing students' ability to identify letters read aloud
- **Sight Word Recognition** (30 items), assessing students' knowledge of high-frequency sight words
- **Nonsense Word Decoding** (30 items), assessing pure decoding in a decontextualized setting

HMH *Phonics Inventory* (continued)

How *The Phonics Inventory* Works

Practice Test

The Phonics Inventory begins with a series of 11 items that give students a chance to "warm up." The student is presented with a series of four circles and is instructed to click on the one that is different as quickly as possible. The student may pause the test, if necessary, by clicking the *Pause* button.

The student's performance on this task is used to ensure that his or her cognitive and/or motor skills do not interfere with the efficacy of the test and to introduce him or her to the test interface.

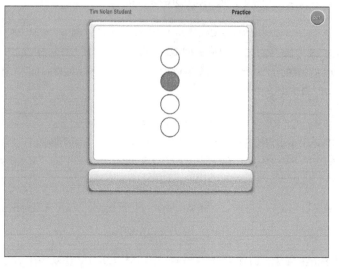

Letter Recognition

The second section of *The Phonics Inventory* consists of 11 items that survey the student's ability to recognize letter names. The student hears a letter name and must click on the corresponding letter from a list of four choices. The test includes lowercase letters as target items and distractors. The student may click the *Replay* button to hear the letter name again. The student may pause the test by clicking the *Pause* button.

The student's performance on this task is used to measure his or her alphabet recognition skills.

Sight Word Recognition

The third section of *The Phonics Inventory* consists of 30 items that assess a student's knowledge of high-frequency sight words selected from the first 300 words on the Dolch and Fry Word Lists. In the first type of activity, the student hears a word and must select the corresponding word from a list of four choices. In the second type of activity, the student hears a high-frequency word and must select the correct spelling from a list of four choices. The student may click the *Replay* button to hear the word again or the *Pause* button to pause the test.

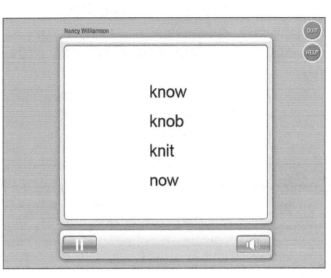

The student's performance on this task is used to measure his or her level of sight word knowledge.

Nonsense Word Decoding

This final section of *The Phonics Inventory* assesses the student's decoding ability using nonsense words: nonwords that follow the conventions of the English language (e.g., *jit, thut, wob*), thereby making them decodable while preventing them from being read from memory. The use of nonsense words is particularly important when testing older struggling readers as many of these students have developed extensive sight word vocabularies that can mask decoding deficiencies. The student may appear to be a fluent reader but still struggle with unfamiliar words that he or she can't decode.

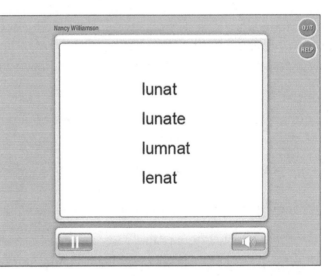

In this section, the student hears a nonsense word and must click on the corresponding word from a list of four choices—all distractors are also nonsense words. The student may click the *Replay* button to hear the word again or the *Pause* button to pause the test. There are 30 items in this section of the test, divided into three subtests of progressive difficulty. The student's performance on this task is used to measure his or her ability to decode in a decontextualized setting.

HMH *Phonics Inventory* (continued)

The Research Behind *The Phonics Inventory*

Overview

The Phonics Inventory was developed under the guidance of Dr. Marilyn Jager Adams, a leader in the field of reading research and instruction, and Dr. Ted Hasselbring of Vanderbilt University, a pioneer in the use of technology in education.

Dr. Richard K. Wagner of the Florida Center for Reading Research devised the scoring algorithm and evaluated the reliability and validity of *The Phonics Inventory*. Dr. Wagner's work is based on analyses conducted with 192 ninth graders in the Southwest, 217 fifth, seventh, and ninth graders in the Southeast, and 182 seventh and eighth graders in the Northeast.

Scoring

The Phonics Inventory measures both the accuracy and fluency of student responses. A response is scored as "accurate" if the student selects the correct answer; it is scored as "fluent" if the student selects the correct answer within the established time limit for the item, known as the fluency threshold.

Fluency thresholds were determined empirically for each item by analyzing the response times of students known to differ in levels of decoding and word recognition. The thresholds were set to optimize differentiation between students with weaknesses in decoding and word recognition and those with adequate decoding and word recognition skills.

Reliability

Reliability refers to the degree to which an assessment produces consistent scores. Two types of reliability were measured for *The Phonics Inventory*.

Internal consistency reliability refers to the degree to which all items in a test measure the same thing. Internal consistency reliability coefficients for the three forms of *The Phonics Inventory* range from .85 to .86, the highest possible value being 1.0.

Alternate-form reliability refers to the consistency of scores produced by different test forms. Alternate-form immediate reliability coefficients for *The Phonics Inventory* range from .78 to .86. The magnitude of these results supports both the internal consistency of *The Phonics Inventory* and the equivalence of the three test forms.

Validity

Validity refers to whether an assessment measures what it claims to measure. Several types of validity are relevant to *The Phonics Inventory*.

- **Content Validity:** Does the test content represent the scope of knowledge or skills being measured?
- **Construct Validity:** Does the test measure the theoretical construct it is supposed to measure?
- **Criterion-Related Validity:** Does the test predict the behavior or performance it is intended to predict?

Content Validity

The Phonics Inventory assesses three foundational reading skills. The items in each test form represent the scope of these skills.

- **Letter Recognition:** All 26 letters of the alphabet are represented, either as targets (correct answers) or distractors (incorrect answer choices). Only lowercase letters are used, as they are generally considered more challenging than uppercase letters and more appropriate for assessing older readers.

- **Sight Word Reading:** In some items, the targets come from the first 300 words on the Dolch and Fry Word Lists and the distractors are common words that look similar to the target. In other items, the targets come from the first 5,000 words in the *American Heritage Word Frequency Book*—a comprehensive list of words found in grade school texts—and the distractors are misspellings of the target.

- **Decoding:** All answer choices are nonwords that follow the conventions of English. The items represent the breadth of spelling patterns taught in most phonics programs and align to the *System 44* scope and sequence. Targets and distractors work together to assess individual sound-spellings and require students to attend to differences among spelling patterns. The items were carefully generated to avoid proper nouns, Spanish words, nonwords that sound like real words, and items that may be difficult for speakers of certain dialects, including African American vernacular English, to distinguish phonologically.

Throughout the development process, all items were reviewed by an esteemed group of reading and assessment experts, and replacements were made as necessary to ensure content validity.

Construct Validity

The Phonics Inventory was examined for construct validity by evaluating whether the test effectively distinguishes between students who are known to differ in levels of decoding and word recognition.

To accomplish this, Dr. Wagner compared differences in *Phonics Inventory* performance to differences in performance on comparable measures—the Sight Word Efficiency and Phonetic Decoding Efficiency subtests of the *Test of Word Reading Efficiency* (TOWRE) and the Letter-Word Identification and Word Attack subtests of the *Woodcock-Johnson III Tests of Achievement*—for a group of students identified as poor decoders and a group of students identified as adequate decoders.

The two groups of students were found to differ substantially and significantly on all three forms of *The Phonics Inventory*. Moreover, the magnitude of these differences exceeded those of both the TOWRE and the Woodcock-Johnson.

HMH *Phonics Inventory* (continued)

Criterion-Related Validity

To examine the criterion-related validity of *The Phonics Inventory*, students' *Phonics Inventory* fluency scores were correlated to their scores on the TOWRE and the Woodcock-Johnson. Correlations ranged from .50, which is acceptable, to .85, indicating that *The Phonics Inventory* is as effective as comparable measures at determining a student's level of decoding and word reading proficiency.

Test Accommodations

The Phonics Inventory offers accuracy-only scoring for students who are unable to manipulate a mouse efficiently due to motor impairments, attention difficulties, or other issues. Teachers can enable this feature for individual students in HMH Teacher Central. For instructions, see *HMH Teacher Central Settings and Reports for The Phonics Inventory*, available online at www.hmhco.com/pi/productsupport.

About Accuracy-Only Scoring

The Phonics Inventory measures both the accuracy and fluency, or speed, of student responses. This facilitates identification of students who lack decoding and word recognition skills, as well as those who possess certain skills but cannot apply them efficiently enough to support comprehension. Students must respond correctly within a given time limit to earn credit for each item.

Students who are unable to manipulate a mouse efficiently due to motor impairments or other issues require special administration of the test so that response time does not adversely affect their scores. You may activate accuracy-only scoring to allow a student's score to be based only on the accuracy of his or her responses. The number and types of test items remain the same. Depending on how difficult it is for the student to move a mouse, you may choose to have an assistant do this for him or her.

The decision to use accuracy-only scoring should be made by the student's teacher or someone who is knowledgeable of the student's ability to manipulate a mouse. **Note that scores based on accuracy alone are not as predictive as those based on accuracy *and* fluency. Enable this feature only when a student is unable to manipulate a mouse efficiently.**

For details about the reliability and validity of accuracy-based scores, see *The Phonics Inventory Technical Guide*, available online at www.hmhco.com/pi/productsupport.

How *Phonics Inventory* Results Are Reported

Individual student results on *The Phonics Inventory* are reported through the Data Dashboard in the Phonics Proficiency and Growth Report. The report indicates the appropriate entry level for decoding instruction for each student.

HMH **TEACHER CENTRAL** Welcome Back, **Jennifer Sloan** ▼

READ 180 – Class 1 ▼ | ⊞ Class Management | ⊿ **Data Dashboard** | ✗ Teacher Tools | 📖 Bookshelf | 🗐 Resources | ⊙ TEACH

Phonics Proficiency & Growth Report
Class 1

🖶 Print Report   ⓘ Learn More   9/15/16 — 10/15/16 ▼

Summary
This report shows changes in performance and progress on the *Phonics Inventory* assessment over time.

15 ⓘ	**3**	**2**
Average PI Fluency Score Growth	Students Improved Their PI Fluency Score	Students Showed No Growth

Performance Level Breakdown

First Test
- 0% / 0 students
- 20% / 3 students
- 46% / 7 students
- 33% / 5 students
- 0% / 0 students

Last Test
- 6% / 1 student
- 27% / 4 students
- 40% / 6 students
- 20% / 1 students
- 6% / 1 student

■ Advancing   ■ Developing   ■ Beginning   ■ Pre-Decoder   ■ No Test Data

> **Performance Level Breakdown** compares the results of the first and last test administrations and displays the percentage change for each decoding status level.

> **Decoding Status** identifies a student as a Pre-, Beginning, Developing, or Advancing Decoder.

Name ∧	Grade ∨	First Test				Last Test		
		Test Date ∨	PI Fluency Score ∨	PI Decoding Status ∨		Test Date ∨	PI Fluency Score ∨	PI Decoding Status ∨
Chu, Amy	7	9/1/15	9	● Pre-Decoder		9/1/15	24	● Advancing
Krynski, Theo	7	9/4/15	21	● Developing		9/4/15	30	● Advancing
Collins, Chris	7	9/2/15	8	● Beginning		9/2/15	14	● Developing
Ramirez, Gabriella	7	9/4/15	13*	● Beginning		9/4/15	13*	● Beginning

SPI Fluency Score	SPI Decoding Status	Recommended Instruction
0-10	● Pre-Decoder	Phonemic awareness, letter names, letter-sound correspondence
0-10	● Beginning Decoder	Foundational phonics
11-22	● Developing Decoder	Targeted phonics remediation
23-60	● Advancing Decoder	Vocabulary, comprehension, fluency

SHOW ▶

HMH *Phonics Inventory* (continued)

Criteria for *Phonics Inventory* Decoding Statuses

The Phonics Inventory is a criterion-referenced test. Criterion-referenced results indicate student performance in relation to an established set of skills.

Phonics Inventory reports describe students' foundational reading skills in terms of four levels of Decoding Status. Results are based on the accuracy of student responses in the Letter Names subtest and both the accuracy and fluency (i.e., speed) of student responses in the Sight Words and Nonsense Words subtests. To receive credit for a fluent response, students must select the correct answer within a given time limit. Response time cutoffs differ by item, based on research conducted with students known to differ in levels of decoding and word recognition. For details of the study, see *The Phonics Inventory Technical Guide*, available online at www.hmhco.com/pi/productsupport.

The chart below details the criteria used to establish each Decoding Status for both the fluency- and accuracy-based versions of the test. **Note that scores based on accuracy alone are not as predictive as those based on accuracy and fluency and should only be used when students require test accommodations because they are unable to manipulate a mouse efficiently.**

Decoding Status	Description	General Criteria	Criteria for Accuracy-Only Scoring
Pre-Decoder	A student with little or no knowledge of letter names or letter-sound correspondences.	• *Phonics Inventory* Fluency Score: 0–10 • Letter Names: less than 70% accuracy • Nonsense Words: less than 50% accuracy on items that assess consonants and short vowels	• Accuracy Score: 0–45 • Letter Names: less than 70% accuracy • Nonsense Words: less than 50% accuracy on items that assess consonants and short vowels
Beginning Decoder	A student who can identify letter names but cannot decode fluently.	• *Phonics Inventory* Fluency Score: 0–10 • Letter Names: at least 70% accuracy • Nonsense Words: at least 50% accuracy on items that assess consonants and short vowels	• Accuracy Score: 0–45 • Letter Names: at least 70% accuracy • Nonsense Words: at least 50% accuracy on items that assess consonants and short vowels
Developing Decoder	A student who can fluently decode words with consonants and short vowels but cannot fluently decode more complex words.	• *Phonics Inventory* Fluency Score: 11–22	• Accuracy Score: 46–49
Advancing Decoder	A student who can decode with adequate fluency.	• *Phonics Inventory* Fluency Score: 23–60	• Accuracy Score: 50–60

Multiple Points of Entry

The Student Application allows for multiple and customized points of entry into *System 44* instruction. Instruction in the *System 44* Student Application is divided into 25 Series. Each Series is made up of 5–8 Topics, or lessons. (For a complete listing of Series and Topics, see the Summary of *System 44* Topics in the *Foundational Reading Guide*, on **page 556.** Access it in the Foundational Reading Collection in HMH Teacher Central.)

- **Series 1:** Students who need the full scope of phonics instruction begin with the first software Series.
- **Series 4:** Students who have demonstrated mastery of consonants and short vowels may begin with Series 4.
- **Fast-Tracks:** Students who are placed in Series 4 take one or more Fast-Track assessments to determine an individualized point of entry based on demonstrated proficiency.

Diagnostic Placement

Students take a series of brief skill-checks known as Fast-Tracks at the beginning of each of the 25 Series of instruction excluding 1–3, 24, and 25. These embedded assessments are similar in structure to *The Phonics Inventory*, but are targeted to the specific phonics skills within a Series of the Student App instruction. Fast-Tracks are designed to identify decoding strengths and weaknesses through the use of both nonsense and real word items. Students who demonstrate proficiency in a Topic Fast-Track through it, only spending time on the Topics that require further instruction. This allows ongoing differentiated placement for each student. Students cannot Fast-Track Topics in the Sight Words or Success strands.

Phonics Inventory **Decoding Status determines recommended placement. Pre- and Beginning Decoders start with Series 1. Developing Decoders start with Series 4. Advancing Decoders place into *READ 180*.**

PI Fluency Score	PI Decoding Status
0-10	● Pre-Decoder
0-10	● Beginning Decoder
11-22	● Developing Decoder
23-60	● Advancing Decoder

Exiting *READ 180*

Most schools establish criteria to assess readiness to move beyond the *READ 180* classroom. Some promote students when they reach a certain performance level—for example, reaching their grade-level proficient performance band on *The Reading Inventory*, reaching Level 5 (Stage A) or Level 6 (Stage B and C) in the Student Application, or when students can successfully read grade-level texts as evidenced by their performance in the classroom and/or on measures of reading achievement.

Students may also leave *READ 180* when they change schools or to make way for students with greater need. Following are recommendations for evaluating students' readiness to accelerate within *READ 180* or to exit *READ 180* and to support students who make the transition.

Pacing, Differentiating, and Accelerating

READ 180 students may have a wide range of skills and reading levels. As they respond to the program, students improve at their own rates. For example, some may accelerate through segments on the Student Application but may still be performing below proficient in their grade-level performance band. Others may be successful using the *ReaL Book* during direct instruction but need more practice to transfer strategies they learned to independent reading or to other classes.

For students who enter *READ 180* reading far below grade level, multiple supports provide necessary scaffolding with developmentally appropriate reading tasks. As students begin making reading gains, *READ 180* offers opportunities to accelerate learning and practice applying reading skills to more complex texts. When students make reading gains and demonstrate success with more advanced content, they may be ready to exit *READ 180*.

Using Multiple Measures of Success

HMH recommends using multiple formal and formative measures to help determine a student's readiness to exit *READ 180* and move into grade level or Tier 1 instruction. These measures may include the following:

Data	Look for...	In the...
Lexile Reader Measures	See Spring Exit Recommendations below. Also see Appendix 4 on **page 191** and Appendix 5 on **page 192.**	*Reading Inventory* Lexile Proficiency and Growth report
READ 180 Workshop Assessments	Consistently high scores on the Level b tests	*READ 180* Workshop Assessment Report
Reading Inventory Normative	65th percentile or higher according to Spring Norms	*Reading Inventory* Lexile Proficiency and Growth report; also see page 58
Student Application Results	High scores in comprehension and vocabulary; multiple segments completed quickly and accurately	*READ 180* Student App report
ReaL Book Completion	High scores on *ReaL Book* work	*ReaL Book* Workshop rubric (teacher-completed)
Oral Fluency	Increase in performance	Oral fluency rubric (teacher-completed)
Other Indicators	Student Language Status, Student IEP Status, other measures of reading achievement	District and school-level recommendations

Formative measures may include:

- Digital Teacher's Edition Observe Board formative assessment results
- Observation of skill levels, motivation, attitude, and behavior
- *Reading Counts!* quiz scores
- Number and level of books read or quizzes passed
- *ReaL Book* writing samples and *ReaL Book* projects
- Student self-evaluation

Spring Exit Recommendations (Current School Year)	
Current Grade	**Eligible for Tier 1**
4	740L and Above
5	830L and Above
6	925L and Above
7	970L and Above
8	1010L and Above
9	1050L and Above
10	1080L and Above
11 and 12	1185L and Above
Recommendation	Enroll in Core program

Supporting Students Beyond *READ 180*

When students leave *READ 180*, it is important to place them into supportive classrooms and monitor their progress as they encounter more difficult content and reading materials. To foster continued success after *READ 180*, encourage students to continue choosing books at the appropriate Lexile levels, especially for Independent Reading.

Fostering a Growth Mindset

What Is a Growth Mindset and Why Is it Important?

Growth mindset refers to the idea that people's intelligence and abilities can be developed through dedication, hard work, and targeted practice. Often students who struggle in school have a fixed mindset. Feeling that they are not smart, these students resign themselves to academic failure. Transforming this negative self-perception into a positive growth mindset can lead students to reengage in learning, persevere, and strive for success in an academic learning environment.

Establish the following tenets of growth mindset through classroom interactions and discussions:

- Every student has the capacity to grow and learn.
- Effort is more important than talent when working to master new skills and concepts.
- Determination, resilience, and perseverance are learnable and teachable.
- Mistakes, challenges, and setbacks are an essential part of the learning process.
- The brain is like a muscle; using it makes it stronger.

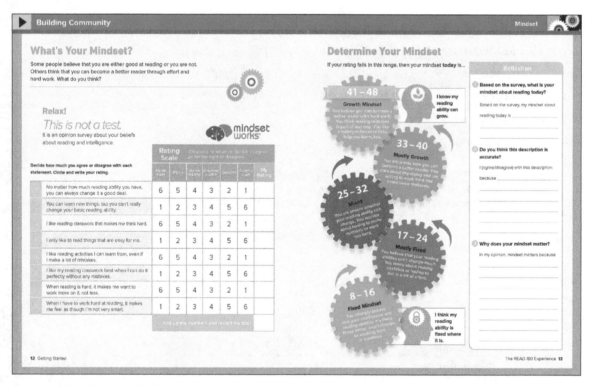

See *ReaL Book* pages 12–15 to have students take a quick survey about mindset and introduce the importance of growth mindset. Then view the Mindset Matters video to show examples and build knowledge.

Develop Academic Mindsets

Use HMH Teacher Central to access and preview the Digital Mindset Scan, an opportunity for students to learn even more about their own mindsets. Ask students to complete the scan after they have learned *READ 180* technology procedures. Use Digital Mindset Scan results to adjust teaching strategies and help students work toward a growth mindset.

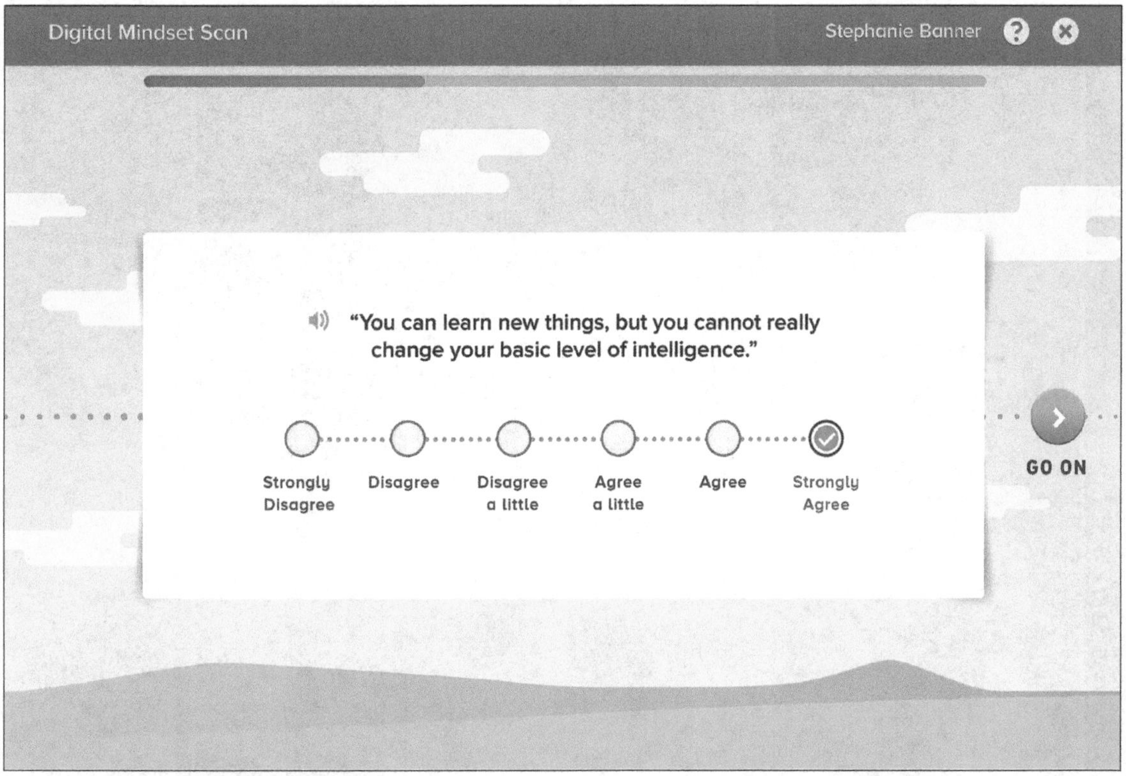

The Digital Mindset Scan provides an opportunity for students to learn even more about their own mindsets.

Providing Feedback

When providing feedback to students, use language that focuses on students' effort and growth, and on the task at hand. Praise students for their hard work and encourage them to learn from mistakes. The following chart provides examples of substituting common feedback for targeted feedback that promotes growth mindset.

Feedback	
Instead of saying...	**Say this**
"Good job!"	"I can see you put a lot of effort into..."
"Sorry, that's not correct."	"It is not correct yet. Let's look at the parts that were difficult."
"You'll do better next time."	"I expect you to make mistakes. Every mistake is a chance to learn."
"This is a tough one."	"Though this may seem challenging, I know you will learn it."

READ180®

Assessment & Analytics Guide

Houghton Mifflin Harcourt.

Progress Monitoring

Curriculum-Embedded Assessment

Oral Fluency Assessment

Data-Driven Instruction

Assessment for Learning

Data Analytics & Communication

Progress Monitoring

This section explains how the Student Application and Independent Reading rotations promote the development of higher-order cognitive skills. Learn how the embedded assessments for these rotations continuously monitor students' comprehension of complex text and question types.

Effective Assessment for Struggling Readers

Regularly monitoring assessment results ensures that all students are on track for success. Use results to monitor students' performance throughout the year, track response to intervention, identify individual strengths and challenges, and target instruction to meet each student's needs. This will ensure that all students are on track for success.

Types of Assessment

To gain a complete picture of what students understand and can do, it is important to consider results from multiple forms of assessment. The type of assessment to use at any given time depends on the assessment goals, such as evaluating overall reading growth or identifying particular focus skills for Small-Group Learning.

Formal and formative assessments allow teachers to evaluate student reading progress and performance. Formal assessment usually involves testing in an effort to produce quantifiable data. Formative assessment includes daily appraisal of a student's progress. When used in tandem, formal and formative assessments provide a comprehensive picture of a student's skill mastery and inform instruction by helping to target areas of weakness.

Assessments in *READ 180*

READ 180 provides continuous assessment and immediate feedback for teachers and students. Formal and formative assessments in *READ 180* are powerful tools for initial screening, placement, and progress monitoring.

Assessment data is fed into HMH Teacher Central, which continuously gathers data and tracks learning gains for each student. These results are detailed in a variety of reports. Results are also captured on Student Central and Leader Central.

In addition to formative assessment, there are four other types of assessment in *READ 180*:

1. Screening and Placement

2. Progress Monitoring

3. Curriculum-Embedded

4. Summative

This section provides an overview of the core assessments included in *READ 180*—what they are, when to use them, what they assess, and how to use the results to plan instruction.

Continuous Assessment

READ 180 includes assessments to help inform instruction and track performance in each area of the Instructional Model.

Begining of Year	During the Year	End of Year
Screening and Placement	**Progress Monitoring, Curriculum-Embedded, Summative**	**Progress Monitoring, Summative**
• HMH *Reading Inventory*	• HMH *Reading Inventory* • *READ 180* Student Application • *System 44* Student Application • *READ 180* Workshop Assessments • *Reading Counts!* Quizzes • *ReaL Book* • *ReaL Book* Performance Tasks • Oral Fluency Assessment	• HMH *Reading Inventory* • *System 44* Progress Monitoring and Summative Assessments • Oral Fluency Assessment

HMH *Reading Inventory* This assessment uses the Lexile Framework as a screening and diagnostic tool to place students appropriately. *The Reading Inventory* provides criterion- and norm-referenced comprehension test results for instructional planning, intervention, and progress monitoring.

***READ 180* Student Application** Each day, students access leveled reading passages that include varying levels of computer support. Students complete work in six zones of the Student App. Assessments are embedded in each zone. Results can be used for diagnostic, instructional planning, intervention, and progress monitoring.

***READ 180* Workshop Assessments** Administer the Interim Assessment at the end of Part 1 and the End-of-Workshop Assessment at the end of each *ReaL Book* Workshop to monitor student performance and understanding of key standards-aligned strategies taught during Whole-Group and Small-Group Learning. Data can be used for intervention, instructional planning, and progress monitoring.

Reading Counts! Through computerized quizzes, *Reading Counts!* provides information to help monitor student comprehension of books and eReads completed during the Independent Reading rotation. Data can be used for intervention, motivation, and progress monitoring.

ReaL Book Students complete daily instructional tasks, such as reading comprehension, vocabulary and word study, writing, and projects. Use Observe Board in Teacher Tools and the rubric results to monitor understanding of whole-group and small-group lessons and pace instruction accordingly.

Oral Fluency Assessments Oral Fluency Assessments may be administered three times a year to monitor student decoding and fluency. Data can be used for intervention, instructional planning, and progress monitoring.

HMH *Reading Inventory*

Using *The Reading Inventory* for Progress Monitoring

READ 180 begins with a screening and placement assessment called *The Reading Inventory* that provides results to identify intervention needs and place students in the appropriate *READ 180* level. Through appropriate screening and placement, students build skills and practice reading with texts that match their individual reading levels.

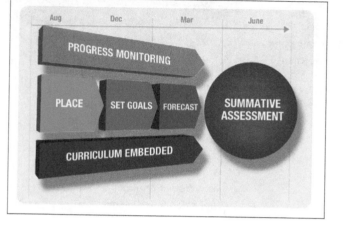

Use *The Reading Inventory* to screen and place students in *READ 180,* monitor reading growth throughout the year, plan differentiated instruction to meet changing needs, and match readers to appropriately leveled texts.

What *The Reading Inventory* Measures

Reporting on a developmental scale, *The Reading Inventory* supports universal screening for all instructional levels. *The Reading Inventory* measures a reader's ability to comprehend narrative and expository texts of increasing difficulty. *Reading Inventory* results help locate a reader's comprehension level on the Lexile Framework, which measures readers and texts using the same scale. Once a reader's comprehension level is measured, it is possible to forecast how well the reader will comprehend reading materials that have also been measured with the Lexile Framework. Use results to establish growth goals and track progress over time as additional *Reading Inventory* tests are administered to students.

Establishing a *Reading Inventory* Testing Cycle

The Reading Inventory can be administered at any time within the school year. The test is untimed. Typically, students take 20–30 minutes to complete the test. Most classrooms choose to administer *The Reading Inventory* during the Student Application rotation. Alternately, schools with a computer lab may utilize the lab to administer *The Reading Inventory* to the entire class simultaneously. If students do not complete the test by the end of the rotation, they may exit out of the software and resume the test the next day.

It is recommended that *READ 180* students take *The Reading Inventory* three to five times each year, with each test administration at least 30 days apart. Spacing the assessments this way allows time between tests for students to make gains through instruction and practice and for teachers to make informed instructional decisions.

Sample *Reading Inventory* Testing Administration Cycle

The chart below provides a sample of an annual *Reading Inventory* testing cycle.

Test	Time of Year	Purpose
1	First three weeks of instruction	Determine initial placement
2	Fall	Close growth monitoring
2	Winter	Forecast annual growth
4	Spring	Summative assessment

Establishing *Reading Inventory* Testing Windows

In addition to establishing the total number of *Reading Inventory* administrations for a school year, schools and districts often establish testing "windows"—specific periods of time to administer each round of *Reading Inventory* testing. Establishing a range of testing dates for each *Reading Inventory* administration enables teachers and students to prepare for an optimal testing experience and address any challenges that may occur with the testing experience.

Establishing school- or district-wide testing windows also ensures that accurate growth comparisons can be made. Many schools and districts establish common testing windows of two to four weeks.

Understanding *Reading Inventory* Growth Targets

As students develop stronger comprehension skills, their reading growth is reflected in their *Reading Inventory* results. When readers are young or just learning to read, their growth rate will be higher. As they become fluent, the rate of growth decreases. For example, when you were learning to read, you likely made large gains in reading comprehension initially. Now that you are a fluent reader, your gains are likely very small.

Understanding *Reading Inventory* Growth Expectations

Determining appropriate growth expectations depends on the student's grade level and current Lexile score. The expected growth rate chart below is based on students whose results indicate that they are reading at the 25th percentile.

Grade	Average Annual Lexile Growth (Based on Students at the 25th Percentile)
3–5	140L
6–8	70L
9–11	50L

When implemented with fidelity, *READ 180* students often exceed average annual growth. Students with lower initial Lexile scores may take longer to reach proficiency. Compare students' initial Lexile and grade-level growth expectations to determine how much growth is needed and the length of time it may take for students to reach proficiency.

HMH *Reading Inventory* (continued)

How *Reading Inventory* Results Are Reported

Teachers administer *Reading Inventory* tests throughout the school year to monitor student progress. Results can be compared against the original (norm) group that took the test. The Lexile Proficiency and Growth report displays *Reading Inventory* results with the following metrics:

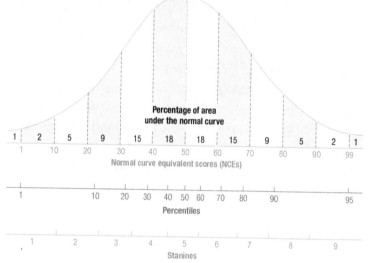

Percentile Rank A student's percentile rank is a score that tells the percent of students in a particular group that received lower scores on a test than the student did. It shows the student's relative position, or rank, in a group of students who are in the same grade. For example, if a student scores at the 65th percentile, it means that the student performed as well or better than 65 percent of the norm group.

Stanine A stanine is a standardized score ranging from 1 to 9. Unlike percentile rank, stanine scores are equally distributed across the entire bell curve for all grade levels. Stanines represent a range of scores. Stanines 1–3 are considered below average, stanines of 4–6 are considered average, and stanines of 7–9 are considered above average. Like percentiles, stanines indicate a student's standing in comparison with the norm group.

Normal Curve Equivalent (NCE) The NCE is a way of measuring where a student falls along a normal bell curve. NCE's range from 1 to 99. If a student was to make exactly one year of progress after one year of instruction, his or her NCE score would remain the same and his NCE gain would be zero, even though his Lexile would increase. Students who make more than a year's progress will have made a larger gain, resulting in a larger NCE score.

Grade Level The grade level indicates how close to grade-level proficiency a student's reading level is, based on his or her Lexile score and associated grade-level Lexile range. Grade-level equivalencies range from Far Below Grade Level to Far Above Grade Level.

Performance Standard A performance standard associates a student's Lexile score with one of four performance standards: Below Basic, Basic, Proficient, and Advanced. These performance standards include a range of Lexile reader measures that vary by grade level.

Variations in *Reading Inventory* Results

It is expected that over the course of the year, students' Lexile scores will increase. Declines in scores between *Reading Inventory* administrations may be based on a variety of factors.

External Factors

- The student's state of mind at the time of testing can affect the test score.
- The student may be tired, hungry, or distracted during an administration, which can impact performance.
- The testing environment may not be conducive for the student. If the classroom environment is noisy or the student feels pressured to complete the test within a set time period, the environment may impact performance.

Internal Factors

- Targeting a *READ 180* student's initial reading level as Basic or Below Basic in HMH Teacher Central enables the test to set initial questions at the appropriate reading level. If a student is significantly below the 50th percentile and is not targeted, it may take longer than one test administration for *The Reading Inventory* to adapt the difficulty of the questions to the students' appropriate level.
- Since *The Reading Inventory* is adaptive, retesting the student too often diminishes the accuracy of *The Reading Inventory* score. Retaking *The Reading Inventory* several times in rapid succession will continue to reduce the possible Lexile gains that a test may reflect, since the gain from item to item gets smaller and smaller with each test within the 30-day window. Severe over-testing can lead to miniscule maximum gains between items, which means that a student's final score could be the same from test to test, regardless of increased performance.

Test...	This may be due to...	HMH recommends...
...shows a slight decline or flatlines.	...the test adapting to a student's true reading level.	...reviewing the test score in context of the student's overall *Reading Inventory* performance. ...waiting for the next *Reading Inventory* testing window to administer another test.
...shows a decline on the second *Reading Inventory* test.	...not appropriately targeting the initial *Reading Inventory* test.	...deleting the initial score in the *Reading Inventory* settings in HMH Teacher Central Assignment Board. ...using the 2nd *Reading Inventory* score as the fall benchmark.
...shows a decline of more than 60 Lexile points and the tests have been administered at least 30 days apart.	...external factors affecting a student's test experience.	...deleting the initial score in the *Reading Inventory* settings in HMH Teacher Central Assignment Board. ...retesting the student within the established testing window.
...shows a decline of more than 60 Lexile points and the tests have been administered less than 30 days apart.	...overtesting.	...establishing testing windows that are at least 30 days apart. ...removing the extra score in the *Reading Inventory* settings in HMH Teacher Central Assignment Board.

READ 180 Student Application

Using Results for Progress Monitoring

The *READ 180* Student App provides individualized instruction and practice using high-interest reading materials and anchored instruction. The Student App presents a carefully planned sequence of instruction and practice activities broken into six zones and continuously assesses and adjusts according to students' skill needs and mastery.

Six Software Zones Continuously Monitor Progress

- Explore Zone
- Reading Zone
- Language Zone
- Fluency Zone
- Writing Zone
- Success Zone

Students receive immediate and encouraging feedback as the Student App gathers information about their proficiency in comprehension, vocabulary, fluency, phonics, spelling, and writing. Use results throughout the year for continuous diagnostic assessment to monitor students' reading progress and group students for targeted instruction.

Understanding Reading Zone Assessments

In the Reading Zone, leveled texts and comprehension tasks offer students adaptive practice with Next Generation item types based on the Depth of Knowledge (DOK) framework. The activities are designed to promote close reading and critical thinking through text-dependent questions that require students to examine the text and cite evidence to support their answers.

Reading Zone Assessment

Core comprehension strategies are built into the leveled texts of the Reading Zone. After listening to a model read of the Anchor Text, students answer questions about the central idea and details of the text. Comprehension task formats include selected response, two-part questions, and text highlighting.

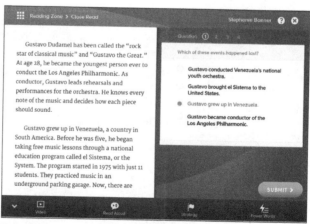

Sample selected-response comprehension task

Close Read Strategies

As students progress through the Reading Zone, they have additional opportunities to reread the Anchor Text. During Close Read, students encounter other comprehension strategies, which may include four of the following:

- Cause and Effect
- Compare and Contrast
- Context Clues (Vocabulary)
- Problem and Solution
- Sequence
- Author's Purpose
- Author's Point of View
- Summary

Close Read builds comprehension through carefully sequenced tasks that progress from literal understanding to higher-order critical thinking. In the second, third, and fourth visits to the Reading Zone, those higher-order thinking skills include: matching, sorting, ordering, and chart completion.

Building Metacognition

To promote success, students have the opportunity to rate their understanding of a text and ability to use a strategy. The Rate activity promotes metacognition as students pause and assess their understanding of a text or strategy, encouraging them to consider why they may be struggling and strategize about how to increase their understanding, or to celebrate their success when they feel they have mastered something.

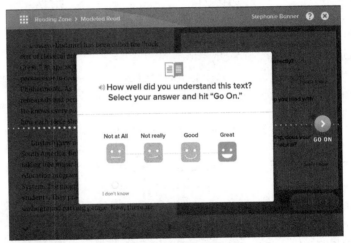

Sample Rate activity from the Reading Zone

Using Reading Zone Results for Instructional Planning

Assessment results are most powerful when used to facilitate instructional planning. Reading Zone results feed reports that appear in the Data Dashboard and can be used to drive instruction in the following ways:

- Use Groupinator recommendations for providing comprehension support at Interim and End-of-Workshop Checkpoints. (See **page 128** for more information on the Groupinator.)
- If a student appears to struggle with a specific comprehension strategy, provide scaffolded support by assigning a Resources for Differentiated Instruction (RDI) lesson.

READ 180 Student Application (continued)

Understanding Fluency Zone Assessments

The Fluency Zone explores the reciprocal nature of decoding and encoding through supportive, engaging activities that provide immediate corrective feedback. Students practice spelling and reading sight words to build automaticity, which allows their cognitive resources to focus on comprehension and retention.

The Spelling activities build spelling and phonics skills. Students receive extra support and instruction, as well as guided and independent practice, culminating in a proofreading activity designed to help them identify and correct misspelled words.

"Pretest" Assessment

The Spelling Assessment helps students see which words from the Assessment List they need to study. Students work with 10 words per round, taken from the Reading Zone passages.

"Post-test" Assessment

In the Spelling Challenge, students hear a word pronounced, then type their spelling of the word. If a word is spelled correctly, students move on to the next word. If a word is misspelled, students receive corrective feedback.

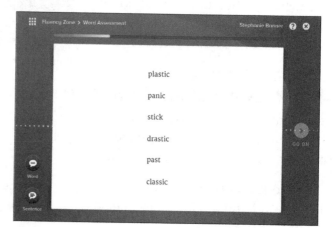

Spelling Assessment

Students receive systematic instruction in decoding and word recognition as they build automaticity. Students work with words included in the Reading Zone passage in an assessment activity, then move on to a study cycle of activities.

"Pretest" Assessment

Students complete a pretest, then receive individualized support and instruction for words they missed or were slow to recognize in the Word Assessment.

"Post-test" Assessment

The Speed Challenge builds students' word recognition and fluency with timed activities for independent practice in identifying Study and Review words.

Word Assessment

Understanding Writing Zone Assessments

After students have completed work in the Fluency Zone, they have the opportunity to respond in writing to their reading. Students will explore the writing process as they plan, organize, write, review, revise, and publish essays.

Writing Zone Options

The Writing Zone is an optional zone that teachers can turn on or off for individual students or the class. Settings may allow students to:

- Complete Writing Zone work for each segment
- Complete Writing Zone work for every other segment
- Go directly to Success Zone

Writing Zone Activities

In the Writing Zone, students practice writing argumentative, informative, and narrative essays. Beginning with a prompt, students are guided through the writing process following a genre-specific strategy. Depending on their level, students are offered various supports: Levels 1 and 2 receive editable sentence frames, Levels 3 and 4 receive editable sentence starters.

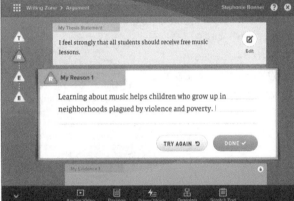

READ 180 Writing Zone: Student App

Students choose a topic or form an argument, support it with descriptions and details, or reasons and evidence, and come to conclusions. Teachers review spelling, grammar, and precision and freshness of expression.

Assessing Writing Zone Responses

Teachers access students' published writing in the Assignment Board on HMH Teacher Central and review the draft and final responses. The structured writing process allows teachers to assess each component of the activity. Score the writing with the accompanying rubric and enter comments.

Assess argumentative writing with the **TREE** rubric (**T**hesis Statement, **R**easons, **E**vidence, and **E**nding). Informative writing is assessed with the **TIDE** rubric (**T**hesis Statement, **I**dea, **D**etails, and **E**nding). Assess narrative essays with the **WWW²H²** rubric (**W**ho, **W**hen, **W**here, **W**hat², and **H**ow²). For every writing type, teacher feedback helps students create well-reasoned and compelling text.

READ 180 Student Application *(continued)*

Understanding Success Zone Assessments

The Success Zone celebrates learning and further challenges students as they integrate and apply skills and vocabulary in new contexts. The Success Zone unlocks once a student has completed all of the other zones. Students working at the upper levels read a stretch text that extends their knowledge of the Segment's topic.

Discrepancy Task

Students read three retellings of the Anchor Text and compare information to select the one that is factually correct. The incorrect information is highlighted. This task requires higher-order thinking skills as students must evaluate new information based on their knowledge of the Anchor Text.

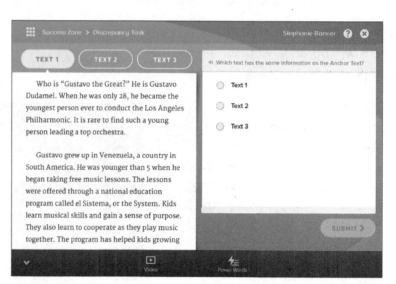

Context Task

The Context Task provides an opportunity for repeated reading as students apply fluency, vocabulary, and comprehension skills to complete a series of cloze texts. (Levels 4–6 do not do this activity.)

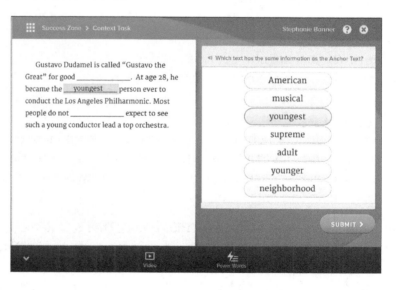

Fluency Check

In the Fluency Zone, students make a final recording of the Anchor Text, which assesses their oral reading fluency. Student have the option to rerecord until they're satisfied with their reading and then submit the recording to their teacher to review. When students compare the final recording to a previous recording in the Reading Zone, the demonstrable gains will boost their confidence and motivate them to continue to work hard.

When students complete their oral fluency practice, their recordings are accessed in the Assignment Board in HMH Teacher Central. Teachers review pronunciation, phrasing, and expression, as students develop word mastery and confidence.

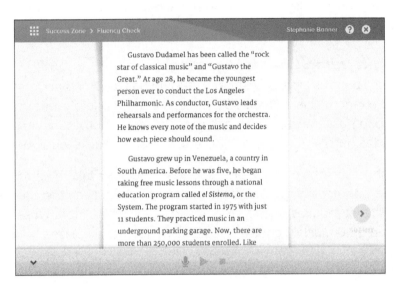

Stretch Read

For students who have completed the Reading Zone at Levels 4–6, a more complex alternative text is provided. This task promotes close reading and critical thinking through text-dependent questions that require students to examine the text and cite evidence to support their answers.

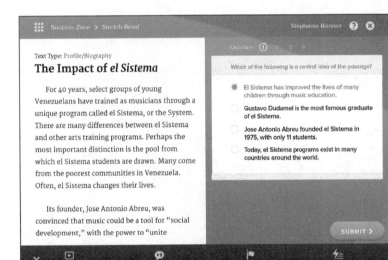

Independent Reading

Reading Counts!

In *READ 180* Universal, *Reading Counts!* quizzes are embedded in the student digital bookshelf, providing resources to assess student progress in the Independent Reading rotation. *Reading Counts!* is based on the positive correlation between reading practice and reading achievement.

Purpose of *Reading Counts!* Quizzes

Reading Counts! quizzes assess whether a student has read and understood a book, audiobook, or eRead article. If students are reading appropriately leveled books, they should be able to pass the quizzes and their success will motivate them to read more. The program includes quizzes for all *READ 180* eBooks, paperbacks, audiobooks, and eReads.

After completing each book, audiobook, or eRead, students take a *Reading Counts!* quiz to demonstrate understanding of what they read. They are given the choice to take a Challenge Quiz that requires higher-order thinking and offers more Quiz Points. Each book quiz is made up of 10 multiple-choice questions while eRead quizzes have five questions.

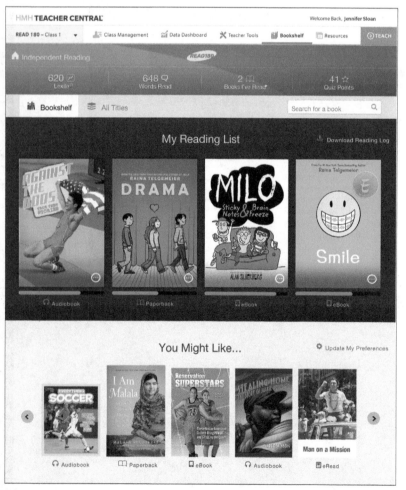

During the daily Independent Reading rotation, students access the Bookshelf to choose and read texts.

How *Reading Counts!* Quizzes Work

Familiarize your students with the format of *Reading Counts!* before they take their first quiz. You may want to review and model strategies for choosing quizzes and answering different types of questions.

When taking a quiz, students:

- Choose a *Reading Counts!* Quiz or Challenge Quiz. Each quiz has five or 10 items.
- Answer questions
- See highlighted answer choices that allow students to check their answer selection before moving on to the next question
- View a results screen upon passing the quiz
- Have the option to review their answers
- Retake a different version of the quiz (the next day) if they score below 70 percent on 10-question quizzes, 60 percent on 5-question quizzes.
- Are not required to complete a quiz in one session. When they return, they will be directed to the first unanswered quiz question.

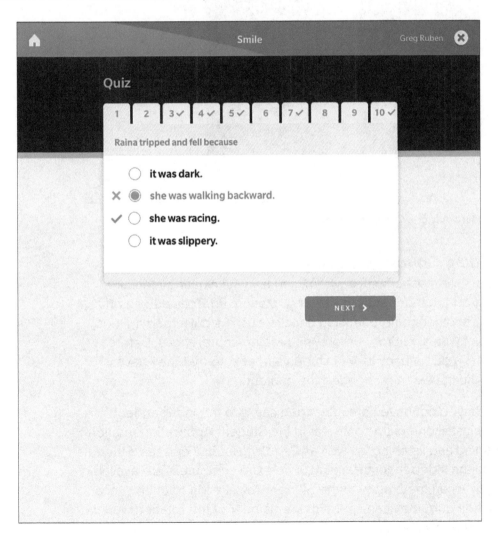

Independent Reading (continued)

What *Reading Counts!* Quizzes Assess

Reading Counts! quizzes enable students to demonstrate comprehension of the books, audiobooks, and eReads they read in the Independent Reading rotation.

Each title has three associated quizzes—two standard quizzes and a Challenge Quiz. Each quiz includes five or 10 multiple choice questions, depending on whether the title is a book or a short eRead article.

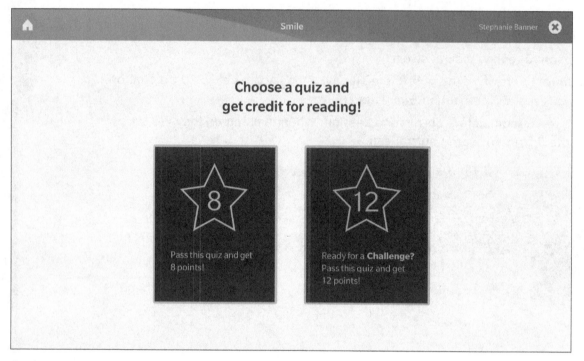

Students can choose a standard quiz or a Challenge Quiz.

When to Use *Reading Counts!* Quizzes

Reading Counts! quizzes are most effective when used as a culminating measure of written accountability for the Independent Reading rotation. Prior to taking a quiz, students should complete other comprehension checks, such as daily reading logs, graphic organizers, QuickWrites, and/or one-on-one reading conferences. Before allowing students to take a quiz, check in with students to ensure that they have completed their book and have comprehended the content.

For those classrooms that do not have computers dedicated to the Independent Reading rotation, many install one extra computer in the Student Application rotation to be used for digital reading and listening, as well as *Reading Counts!* quizzes. Students can then take a quiz during Independent Reading. If no extra computers are available, students can take a quiz when they rotate to the Student Application rotation. Once they have completed their quiz, they can spend the remainder of the rotation working on the *READ 180* Student Application.

Using *Reading Counts!* for Progress Monitoring

Reading Counts! quizzes enable monitoring of student progress in the Independent Reading rotation. *Reading Counts!* analytics provide actionable data that allow for evaluation of student progress in order to raise student achievement.

- Student progress can be tracked by quizzes passed, points earned, and/or words read.
- Student progress can be evaluated by an increase in Lexile score, performance standard, or other normative data.
- Student progress can be measured against quantifiable reading goals that are customizable in HMH Teacher Central.

Using the Data Dashboard to Monitor Student Progress

Access the Independent Reading Reports from the Data Dashboard of HMH Teacher Central to track student progress based on *Reading Counts!* data and activity on the Student Bookshelf.

The Class Independent Reading report tracks total *Reading Counts!* quizzes passed as well as other information about the kinds of texts students are reading.

Independent Reading *(continued)*

Using *Reading Counts!* for Student Motivation

Establishing manageable goals and tracking progress toward reaching those goals facilitate student engagement in the classroom. For struggling readers who may have experienced frustration or failure with reading in the past, employing goals for independent reading is especially important.

Reading Counts! provides a structured system to manage and track individual student goals. Progress toward achieving these goals can be tracked for individuals, groups, classes, or schools.

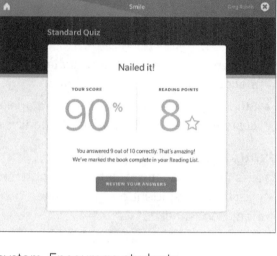

Establish an incentive system for words read, books read, quizzes passed, or Quiz Points earned. Use results for groups or classes as part of an incentive or motivation system. Encourage students to review *Reading Counts!* progress on Student Central. As students experience reading success and see results tracked, they build the confidence necessary to attempt new and more complex reading challenges.

Motivation and Incentive Systems

There are a variety of ways to use *Reading Counts!* to establish a classroom motivation system. Some possibilities include:

Words Read

- Highlight the top students each month.
- Compete for top group or class each grading period.
- Establish increasing goals of total words read each grading period for each student.
- Collaborate with other *READ 180* classrooms to attempt 1,000,000 words read by the end of the year.

Quizzes Passed/Quiz Points Earned/Books Read

- Highlight the top students each grading period.
- Compete for top group or class each grading period.
- Establish increasing goals each grading period for each student.

Consider celebrating by inviting the principal or other administrator to read with students during the Independent Reading rotation. Access the HMH Certificate Tool http://educatorcommunity.hmhco.com/resources/article/classic-certificate-tool to recognize reading achievement.

Establishing Independent Reading Goals

Reading Counts! can be used to establish and track annual student goals for independent reading. Goals can be set for texts read and points earned when students pass quizzes. Students can develop stronger skills and fluency by extending their range of reading, trying books with higher Lexile measures, and taking challenge quizzes.

Teachers can begin the goal-setting process by reviewing the *READ 180* Independent Reading guidelines below. Individual goals will accommodate student skills and interests while encouraging new reading experiences and increasing background knowledge.

Most *READ 180* students can be expected to read between eight and 12 pages during each Independent Reading rotation. The values are approximate.

Stage	Daily Number of Pages	End of Year Goal (Standard and Challenge Quiz Points)	End of Year Goal (Texts)
A	8-10	150-175	8 fiction + 6 nonfiction + 10 eReads
B	10-12	175-200	9 fiction + 8 nonfiction + 15 eReads
C	10-12	200-225	10 fiction + 10 nonfiction + 15 eReads

Other Independent Reading Assessments

Regular written accountability is also an integral component of daily progress monitoring of student participation and comprehension of readings completed independently. There are multiple ways to regularly monitor and assess student work completed in the Independent Reading rotation.

Daily Reading Logs

Daily reading logs help students maintain focus and synthesize information from daily reading. Incorporating daily reading logs into your assessment plan helps make students more accountable. Check reading logs each day so that students can receive immediate feedback.

Implementing and Assessing Daily Reading Logs

1. In HMH Teacher Central, go to Resources and download and make copies of the Daily Reading Log.

2. Distribute blank reading logs during Whole-Group Learning at the beginning of each week.

3. Have students predate reading logs for the week.

4. Alert students during the last 1–2 minutes of the rotation that they should complete their reading log, or allow students to spend the first 1–2 minutes of Small-Group Learning completing their reading logs while you assist the other groups in properly beginning rotations.

5. Quickly review daily reading logs at the beginning of Small-Group Learning. Check for completion of work and total pages read, and initial the log if expectations are met.

6. Complete a more thorough review of the reading log once a week or as students complete each book or eRead.

Graphic Organizers and QuickWrites

There are additional resources to track student progress and comprehension during Independent Reading. Graphic Organizers and QuickWrites are available for all eBooks, paperbacks, and audiobooks. Access Independent Reading support materials from **Resources** on HMH Teacher Central.

Graphic Organizers

Students can complete graphic organizers as they progress through their books or audiobooks. Schedule time to review their progress as they read their books, and review the graphic organizer for accuracy before students take a *Reading Counts!* quiz. Teachers can download and print each graphic organizer from **Resources** on HMH Teacher Central.

QuickWrites

Like graphic organizers, students can also complete QuickWrites as they progress through their books or eReads. Schedule time to review their progress as they read their book, and review all of their QuickWrites responses for accuracy before they take a *Reading Counts!* quiz.

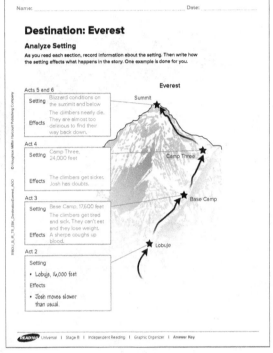

Reading Conferences and Other Methods of Assessment

To monitor student progress and comprehension, you may wish to hold one-on-one student reading conferences. Text Overviews contain conference discussion starters and sample student responses for each book and eRead in the *READ 180* Independent Reading Library.

You may also wish to incorporate other methods of assessing students' independent reading, such as book talks, presentations, or assigning literary analysis as homework.

Structuring Independent Reading Assessment

A strong Independent Reading rotation includes multiple measures of regular accountability and assessment, including:

1. Daily reading logs, assessed for completion daily and for content on a regular basis

2. One or two additional measures of written accountability, such as graphic organizers or QuickWrites

3. *Reading Counts!* quiz, taken when students complete each text

Incorporating these measures of continuous progress-monitoring assessment ensures that students receive the support they need to achieve independent reading success.

READ180®

Assessment & Analytics Guide

Placement & Exiting

Pro Mor

Curriculum-Embedded Assessment

Data-Driven Instruction

Assessment for Learning

Data Analytics & Communication

Houghton Mifflin Harcourt.

Curriculum-Embedded Assessment for Whole- and Small-Group Learning

The *ReaL Book* is the instructional pathway through Whole- and Small-Group Learning. Discover how the curriculum-embedded formative assessments and performance tasks gauge students' progress in meaning making through close reading and critical thinking.

The *READ 180* Blended Learning Model

Whole- and Small-Group Learning

READ 180 Universal features a flexible rotation model designed to help you address students at all levels of intervention. This model organizes class time to provide a balance of teacher-led instruction, scaffolded practice, and small-group interaction. It is designed to maximize instructional time and accelerate achievement. Backed by more than 15 years of research and results, studies confirm that *READ 180* effectively raises reading achievement when students experience all aspects of the blended learning rotation model.

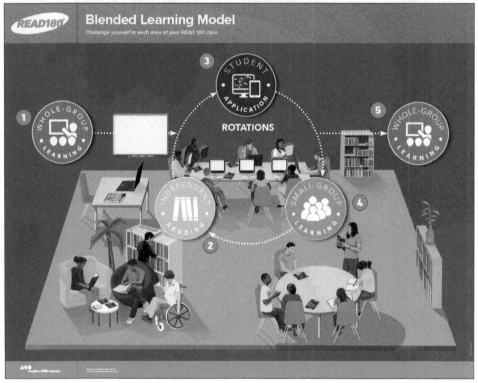

The Blended Learning Model poster

1 Whole-Group Learning
Teachers begin class by facilitating instruction in close-reading strategies, academic vocabulary, writing, and academic discussion.

2 Independent Reading
Students have their choice of engaging, content-rich texts to which they can apply their newly acquired vocabulary and comprehension skills.

3 Student Application
Students work independently on the *READ 180* Student Application, following a personalized path that accelerates their learning.

4 Small-Group Learning
In a small-group setting, students receive targeted, data-driven instruction unique to their individual learning needs while building meaningful relationships with their teacher and peers.

5 Whole-Group Learning
At the end of class, each day's Wrap Up guides students to reflect on the day's learning, mindset, successes, and challenges.

Rotation	Description	Sample Component
WHOLE-GROUP LEARNING	The *ReaL Book*—with an emphasis on **"R"** Reading and **"L"** Language—includes six Workshops with an essential question that drives instruction over four to six weeks.	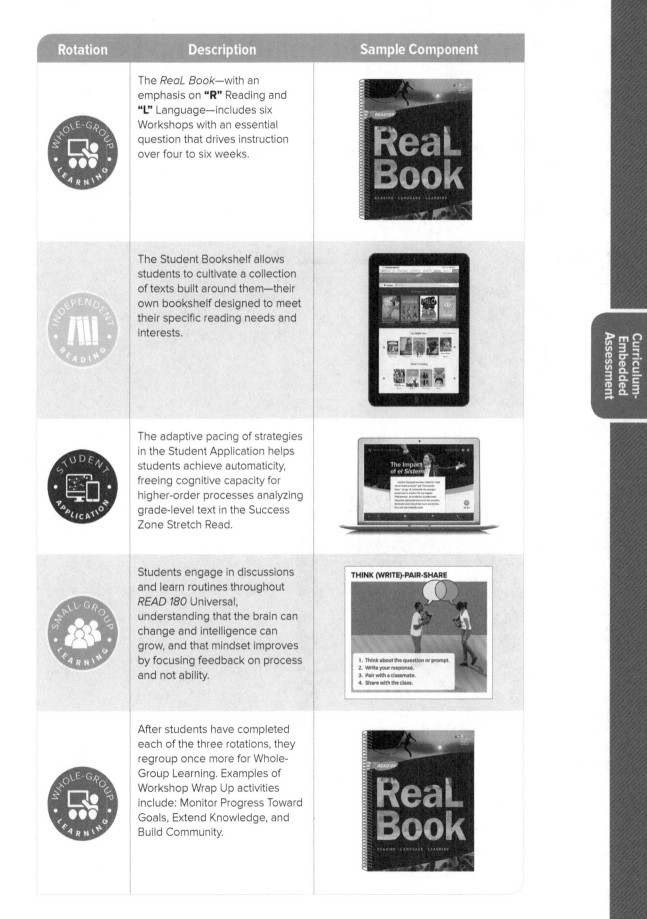
INDEPENDENT READING	The Student Bookshelf allows students to cultivate a collection of texts built around them—their own bookshelf designed to meet their specific reading needs and interests.	
STUDENT APPLICATION	The adaptive pacing of strategies in the Student Application helps students achieve automaticity, freeing cognitive capacity for higher-order processes analyzing grade-level text in the Success Zone Stretch Read.	
SMALL-GROUP LEARNING	Students engage in discussions and learn routines throughout *READ 180* Universal, understanding that the brain can change and intelligence can grow, and that mindset improves by focusing feedback on process and not ability.	**THINK (WRITE)-PAIR-SHARE** 1. Think about the question or prompt. 2. Write your response. 3. Pair with a classmate. 4. Share with the class.
WHOLE-GROUP LEARNING	After students have completed each of the three rotations, they regroup once more for Whole-Group Learning. Examples of Workshop Wrap Up activities include: Monitor Progress Toward Goals, Extend Knowledge, and Build Community.	

Tools for Whole- and Small-Group Learning

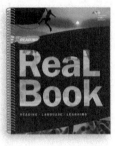

READ 180 Universal provides educators with comprehensive tools to facilitate effective instruction for Whole- and Small-Group Learning.

For Students: The *ReaL Book*

The *ReaL Book* is the students' learning pathway through whole- and small-group instruction. Each of the six *ReaL Book* Workshops are guided by a Focus Question that drives inquiry.

In Print

Students make the *ReaL Book* their own through text marking, writing, and annotating their individual copies.

On Screen

Display the *ReaL Book* via HMH Teacher Central to guide teaching and learning, focus students' attention, and provide adaptive, digitally based supports.

Digital Tools

- Choose to display response frames to scaffold use of academic language.
- Choose when to display answers as models for students.
- Use the markup tool to highlight and circle relevant text evidence.
- Zoom in to focus student attention.

For Teachers

Digital

The *ReaL Book Digital Teacher's Edition* on HMH Teacher Central provides guidance as you plan, teach, assess, and differentiate instruction.

Print

The *Blended Learning Handbook* Lesson Digests present a print option with abridged lessons for quick reference and planning.

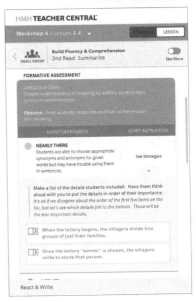

Assess

Integrated Formative Assessment

Each lesson includes two point-of-use Formative Assessments, including support options tied to student proficiency levels. Access the Observe Board tool on HMH Teacher Central to enter Formative Assessment data, so it can be reflected in Data Dashboard reports.

Use the Observe Board tool to assess daily literacy and language goals.

Differentiate

Resources for Differentiated Instruction

Use the resources referenced in each lesson to support, extend, and build language tied to lesson goals.

Meeting Individual Needs

Each text-based lesson includes references to mini-lessons geared for students who need extra guidance with foundational reading skills, English learners, and speakers of African American English. These resources provide targeted language support related to words in the day's text.

Sample Resources for Differentiated Instruction lesson

ReaL Book Workshop Assessments

READ 180 Universal provides curriculum-embedded summative assessments that measure students' literacy skills and help teachers monitor reading progress at key points in the READ 180 Universal program, as well as during the school year.

This section describes the various assessments included in the ReaL Book:

- Formative Assessment
- Portfolio Assessment
- Interim and End-of-Workshop Assessments
- Multimedia Performance Tasks

Formative Assessment

What Are Formative Assessments?

Formative assessments provide timely and specific information that teachers can use to inform or modify ongoing instruction to best meet the immediate needs of the students. Formative assessments are often referred to as assessments for learning, which means that educators evaluate the learning processes themselves to make them the most effective possible.

Key elements in formative assessment include:

- Setting clear, explicit, and specific criteria for goal achievement
- Student understanding and internalizing of learning targets
- Frequent evaluation of where students are in relation to their goals
- Adapting instruction to address student needs
- Peer-assessment: students giving constructive feedback to each other
- Self-assessment: students monitoring their own progress toward learning goals
- Creation of collaborative classroom culture that encourages developing skills and improving together

Clarifying Literacy and Language Goals

Every small-group lesson includes at least two formative assessment moments. Each lesson features a response item such as a Close Reading question that correlates to one of the lesson's goals. As students formulate their response, use the Observe Board to quickly adapt instruction and record each student's mastery of the goal.

Steps for Launching Observe Board

1. While teaching a lesson with the *ReaL Book* Digital Teacher's Edition, navigate to the Small Group section of the lesson. Review the small-group instruction, including the lesson's goals. From the Teacher Tool pull-down, select **Observe Board**.

2. Select **Performance**.

3. Select your current **Workshop.**

4. Select the **Lesson** you are currently teaching.

5. Select **Start Observing** to open the Observe Board. Evaluate each student response against the Observe Board rubric.

6. Select **Adapt Instruction** in each performance band for guidance on adapting instruction.

7. Select a student, then select the appropriate performance level.

The data captured during formative assessment contributes to each student's data profile. Review formative assessment data in the Data Dashboard of HMH Teacher Central.

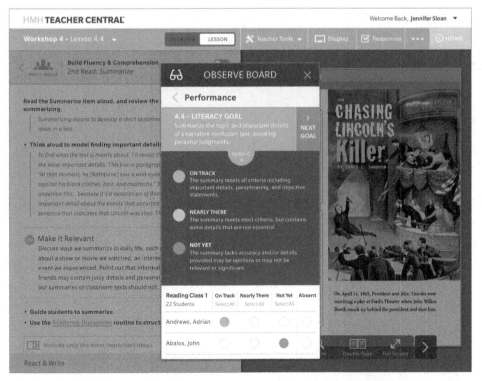

Sample Observe Board rubric from the *ReaL Book* Digital Teacher's Edition

Formative Assessment *(continued)*

Each lesson in the *ReaL Book* Digital Teacher's Edition includes anywhere from two to five literacy and language goals. Share these goals with the class at the beginning of the lesson, and discuss them with students to ensure that they have a clear understanding of the goals. Evaluate students' progress relative to these goals during their work to ensure the learning targets are reached.

HMH TEACHER CENTRAL

Workshop 4 - Lesson 4 ▾   OVERVIEW   LESSON   🛠 Teacher T

< Objectives

Primary Goals

- Literacy Goal: Summarize the topic and important details of a narrative nonfiction text, avoiding personal judgments.
- Language Goal: Engage in collaborative discussions on topics, texts, and issues, clearly expressing personal perspectives.

Additional Goals

- Literacy Goal: Determine the key idea of a text, citing evidence.
- Language Goal: Apply high-utility academic words in example sentences including relevant content and correct grammar.

Scaffolding Tracker

SCAFFOLDING TRACKER: Summarize

TEACH	PRACTICE	APPLY
1.10 1.14	**4.4** 4.17	6.6

You are here

Digital Teacher's Edition: Sample Literacy and Language Goals

The Primary Goals indicate which goals to emphasize. Once students master the priorities of the lesson, begin working on mastering the Additional Goals. Monitor student mastery and tailor instruction to maximize student achievement throughout the formative assessment process.

Identifying Evidence of Learning

The focus of a formative assessment is to evaluate the learning process as it happens, to understand what students have learned and what they need, and then to adjust the teaching strategy to meet those needs. The basis for making those adjustments is the feedback students give during the learning process. Identifying this feedback and interpreting it to determine students' levels is key to successful formative assessment.

Close Reading questions (below right) can be used as an informal assessment of student progress. After students respond, evaluate responses in relation to the learning goal of the assignment. These informal responses are considered *anecdotal evidence*.

Use the **Observe Board** (below left) to interpret the anecdotal evidence of the students' work. Compare their answers to the learning targets to determine the students' level of achievement with regards to the criteria: **On Track**, **Nearly There**, and **Not Yet**.

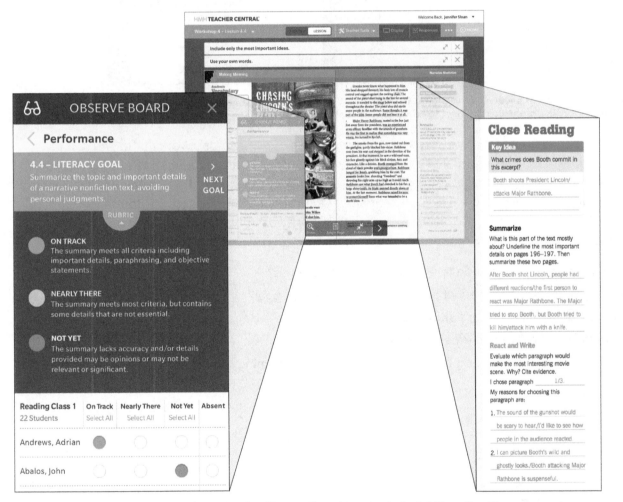

Gather formative assessment results using the Observe Board to rate students' Close Reading responses.

Formative Assessment *(continued)*

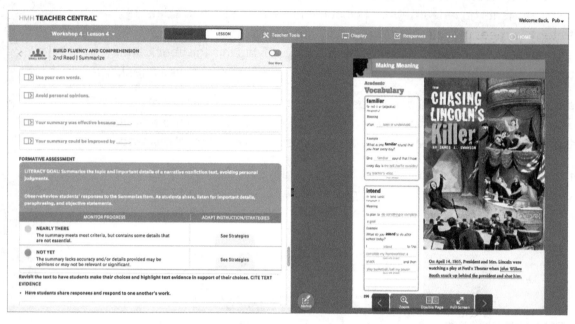

The Formative Assessment section of the Digital Teacher's Edition helps you organize evidence distilled from student responses to decide how best to adapt teaching strategies.

Most evidence used in a formative assessment comes from the day-to-day work in the classroom rather than from a formalized test. Use strategically formatted questions to retrieve relevant answers from students or observe students in classroom discussion. For a more formalized approach, use rubrics or surveys throughout the lesson. Students can also write self-reflections, for example, by journaling. Any assignment or task can be used to gather information on students to determine:

- Where are students in relation to established learning goals?
- What gap is present between where students are and the goal?
- What individual difficulties are students having?
- What patterns of difficulties emerge among students?
- Are any foundational "building blocks" missing from their learning?

Adapting Instruction/Strategies

Once you have gathered sufficient evidence from the students and used the Observe Board to gauge where the students are in relation to their learning goals, begin to adapt instruction and teaching strategies to accommodate student needs.

Monitor Progress displays the rubric criteria: "Nearly There" and "Not Yet." Click "See Strategies" for suggestions on adapting instruction at both levels of achievement.

Instruction must be flexible to accommodate the learning needs of the individual students as well as the needs of the class. Some strategies you can use are:

- Look for patterns of student achievement or needs—determine which concepts are strong and which are lacking or misunderstood.
- Break down goals into smaller "stepping stones."
- Ask questions of students in class to ensure understanding.
- Provide feedback—let students know what they need to work on, and make suggestions to help them improve weak areas.
- Focus on individual needs—conference with individual students, establish short-term goals, then reevaluate to see how the student responds to feedback.

Formative Assessment *(continued)*

Peer- and Self-Assessment

Students can use formative assessments to evaluate their own progress and adjust their learning strategies. Both the assessment of the student by his or her peers and assessment of the student by him- or herself let students actively participate in the learning process. Peer- and self-assessments allow students to examine their work and the work of their peers to develop insight, gain a deeper understanding of learning goals, and generate feedback relative to student progress.

Encourage students to share what they've learned in their own words and invest in the outcome of their learning. Through these assessments, students learn to recognize and articulate challenges, prioritize goals, and strategize to overcome those challenges. As students gain more confidence in their ability to identify and overcome challenges, they will develop a sense of motivation, efficacy, and autonomy that augments their learning.

What Is Peer-Assessment?

Peer-assessment is an active learning process in which students evaluate each other's work. This can be done by all members of a class evaluating a presenter, by group members evaluating each other, or by partners providing feedback on each other's work.

Peer-assessment helps students learn in many ways. Both the act of giving and receiving feedback are useful skills and tools. Receiving feedback from peers helps students to become aware of errors they might have missed in their work or to hear new ideas they might not have thought about. Being able to provide constructive feedback is also a valuable skill. Constructive feedback entails using positive language, making helpful suggestions, and ensuring that any feedback is specific and actionable.

Formative Assessment: Peer Feedback Routine

1. Discuss criteria.

2. Determine self-ratings.

3. Assign partners and have students exchange their drafts.

4. Each partner fills out a rubric and/or a feedback form.

The Peer Feedback Routine suggests steps for constructive peer review.

Name: _____ Date: _____

Peer Feedback and Self-Evaluation Frames

Feedback for Peers
• To make your claim stronger, you could _____.
• Your claim about _____ works well, but _____ needs more support.
• A relevant example of _____ would strengthen your essay.
• To make your writing more interesting to a reader, you could _____.
• Your (thesis / detail / conclusion) _____ is engaging, but _____ could be improved.

essay, it is important to evaluate the
...cture of the essay. Use the sentence frames
...your informative essay and provide feedback

	Feedback for Peers
...ger, I could	• To make your claim stronger, you could _____.
...orks well, ... needs	• Your claim about _____ works well, but _____ needs more support.
___ would	• A relevant example of _____ would strengthen your essay.
...re could	• To make your writing more interesting to a reader, you could _____.
...clusion) ___ could be	• Your (thesis / detail / conclusion) _____ is engaging, but _____ could be improved.

READ180 Universal | Stage B | RDI | Writing | **Check Point**   Page 1 of 1

1   3/18/16 4:08 PM

The right column of this RDI writing graphic organizer provides sentence frames for students to structure their early attempts at peer review.

In the Resources for Differentiated Instruction (RDI) graphic organizer above, students use sentence frames to help them evaluate both strong aspects and areas that need improvement in their partner's work. The exercise allows students to work in pairs without teacher input while still maintaining a level of guidance. The goal is for students to internalize the thought process represented in this graphic organizer and be able to apply it to future peer-assessment exercises without or with less scaffolding.

The act of evaluating a peer's work also helps the student to hone his or her understanding of the criteria against which they will also be evaluated. It provides the student with a sample to evaluate that is less emotional than evaluating the student's own work and, in that way, enables students to be more objective and to clarify the standards in an unbiased manner. Finally, it permits students to internalize the criteria for an assignment during the creative process of the assignment, allowing them to better achieve their learning goals.

What Is Self-Assessment?

Self-assessment is a process for generating internal feedback in which a student sets a goal, strategizes how to achieve that goal, works toward the goal, and then evaluates how far toward the goal he or she has gotten over the course of an assignment or a series of assignments. It should be an ongoing process. This process helps students to develop skills such as setting goals, managing the pursuit of goals, and self-monitoring. It also helps them chart their own course toward learning goals tailored to their specific needs.

The Make It Relevant section in the Digital Teacher's Edition includes concrete steps to help students achieve Literacy Goals.

Self-assessment can be taught from a very young age by helping students to set goals attainable at their level, then asking questions about the goal, such as "*Did you meet your goal? What do you need to do for next time to meet your goal?*"

Setting Goals: The Key to Self-Assessment

Setting goals is at the heart of teaching students to effectively assess themselves. For example, the Digital Teacher's Edition (shown above) provides a framework to set goals with students and illustrates what concrete steps to achieve those goals will look like. Share the overarching goals with students at the beginning of a lesson. Then review the steps enumerated as frequently as is helpful for students to stay on track. By sharing and discussing the goals and the individual steps students will take to attain them, you will help students keep the lesson goals in mind as they work and to begin the internal thought process of evaluating their progress against those goals.

At its most fundamental, self-assessment helps students to become aware of their strengths and weaknesses, then builds on that awareness to develop time management, self-monitoring, and critical-thinking skills. The most effective learners are those who develop these self-regulating skills and are able to apply them in various situations.

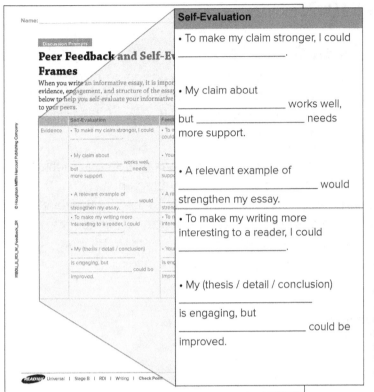

The left column of this RDI writing graphic organizer provides sentence frames for students to structure their early attempts at self-review.

Use Scaffolds to Foster Independence

By providing rubrics, sentence frames, checklists, and/or graphic organizers, you can scaffold students' progress and foster their development of self-regulation skills. For example, the RDI graphic organizer above allows flexibility for students to work independently with the tools provided and familiarizes them with the language and thought process of self-assessment.

In both peer- and self-assessment, the focus of the task is the processes being used for learning and the students' self-regulation. One aim of this technique is to create an environment where making mistakes is okay and correcting them is beneficial to the student's overall development. Students should begin to become aware of their own mistakes, both through peer suggestion and through an amelioration of their own self-awareness.

Establishing a Collaborative Classroom Culture

The focus of peer- and self-assessment is on mastery of skills rather than on achievement of a performance grade. Therefore, students should see each other not as competition but rather as allies or learning partners. The goal of the classroom is that everyone should master the skills being taught. A collaborative culture ideally encourages students to work together to develop each other's skills. Class discussions can be a wellspring of new ideas and using peer review allows students to build on one another's ideas and help their classmates improve. It is important to foster an environment that encourages each student to participate, try hard, and keep growing.

Formative Assessment (continued)

Co-Constructing Rubrics With Students

A rubric articulates the expectations of student performance for an assignment; it states what criteria are being evaluated and concrete points that describe different levels of quality within each criterion. Rubrics make teachers' expectations clear to students and show them concretely in steps how to meet those expectations.

Take student input into consideration during the assessment process by co-constructing the rubric with students. Co-construction builds students' understanding and acceptance of learning expectations. It brings the assessment tools to the student level and takes into account their understanding of the subject matter. It also eliminates the guessing game of "*What's the teacher looking for?*" and instead allows them to share what they know, think critically, and discuss criteria and achievement levels.

How to co-construct a rubric:

1. Define what the expected achievement or objective is.
   Ask: *What is the ideal outcome to achieve or skill to develop?*

2. Show students examples.
   Model *at least three samples of each level.*

3. Brainstorm with students to make a list of their top criteria.
   Ask: *What counts in quality work? Include at least two but no more than six criteria in the final rubric.*

4. Determine the degrees of quality for each criterion.
   Define *the worst and the best levels of achievement for each. Then define the degrees of difference between the middle level(s).*

5. Have students practice evaluating sample papers.
   Use *the rubric they created. This helps them understand each performance level in practice.*

6. Have students use the rubric to peer- and self-assess.
   Make sure *students self-assess before submitting their final product. They should use feedback from peer- and self-assessments.*

7. Grade student work.
   Use *the rubric you co-constructed with your students.*

Co-construction of rubrics is a useful tool that can be applied to any lesson. It is a great way to increase student engagement and participation in the learning process and to help them understand teacher expectations.

HMH Teacher Central logo: For more in-depth learning, access the **Peer- and Self-Assessment Teacher Packet** from **Resources** on HMH Teacher Central.

Skills-Focused Rubric

Student Name: _____ Date: _____

Skills-Focused Rubric

Skills	Goal	Improved	Need to work on
1. Vocabulary • Look up unfamiliar words. • Rewrite definitions of new words in your own words. • Practice using words you rated "1" or "2" in a sentence. • Use a thesaurus to find synonyms for a familiar word. • Make a word map to understand word connections. • Think of two words that mean similar things and tell whether each has a "positive" or "negative" connotation.	My goal is to use three words from the reading that I rated "1" or "2" in a sentence this week	I didn't know the words "assassin," "tyrant," or "emancipate" before I read this text and their definitions. I used all three words in their own sentences this week. Now I have mastered these three words, and I can use them in my writing.	Next time, I want to make a word map to help me understand related words.
2. Comprehension • Identify the central idea of a text and write it in your own words. • Choose two details from a text and tell how they relate to the main idea. • Explain how a character feels based on text evidence. • Explain a cause and effect using details from the text. • Explain how an idea and an event in the text are connected. • Choose a detail and tell how it shows the mood of the text.	My goal is to...	Before, I didn't/couldn't... I did... Now I can...	Next time, I want to...

Above is a sample skills-focused rubric. Use it to focus on improving one or two skills over time. Based on classroom needs, you can modify the skills in the first column, then set goals for developing each skill by brainstorming with students.

When you first introduce this rubric, work with students to fill out the three boxes in the top row along with the listed goals. Provide scaffolding prompts, as shown in the annotations above. As students develop more autonomy in their self-assessment, allow them to fill in the boxes with less help. This rubric can be used with most projects and can be made as comprehensive or as simple as the skill or project requires.

Evaluating and Goal-Setting Rubric

Evaluating and Goal-Setting Rubric
Use the chart below to set a goal for yourself for your next assignment.

Skill	Score	My goal for next time
1. Vocabulary: learning and using new and different words		
2. Comprehension: understanding central ideas and how they connect		
3. Literary Elements: reading deeper meaning in a text and understanding figurative language		
4. Structure: understanding how a text organizes information		
5. Response: answering questions about what you read		
6. Application: writing about what you read		

Use this rubric to encourage self-evaluation and goal setting. With students' help, this type of rubric can ideally be created using the Primary Goals found at the beginning of each Workshop lesson in the Digital Teacher's Edition. Creating this rubric with students will remind them of the goals you discussed at the beginning of the lesson and will allow them to check their understanding of the criteria once more before evaluating themselves against those criteria.

Portfolio Assessment

A portfolio is a collection of work that reflects a student's progress and achievements. You may wish to create separate folders or notebooks for each student in which to file writing samples, observation notes, completed activities from Checkpoints, and written responses completed during Independent Reading.

Compiling Student Portfolios

Artifacts for Student Portfolios may include:
- *READ 180* Workshop Assessment report
- Lexile® Proficiency and Growth report
- Independent Reading report
- *READ 180* Workshop Assessment Student Test Printouts
- *ReaL Book* Writing
- *ReaL Book* Performance Tasks
- Daily reading logs
- Independent Reading QuickWrites and Graphic Organizers
- Oral Fluency Assessment Results

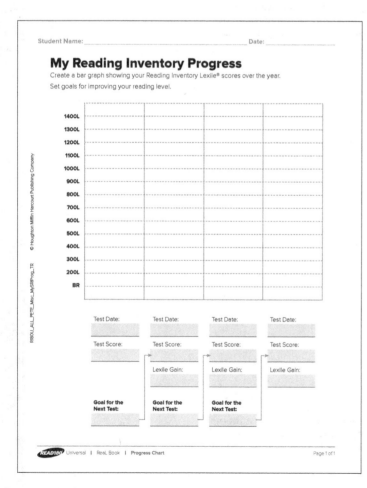

This section will look more closely at three other assessments that can be included in a Student Portfolio:
- *ReaL Book* Writing
- *ReaL Book* Project
- *ReaL Book* Workshop

Use the My Reading Inventory Progress chart to track Lexile growth measures.

Assessing *ReaL Book* Writing

Students complete the writing process in each *ReaL Book* Workshop. Rubrics to assess student writing are available for each *ReaL Book* Workshop. They provide guidance in assessing student writing. As an assessment tool, rubrics offer guidelines to help ensure that all students are assessed on the same scale. They serve as a concrete reference to help determine student grades and explain these grades to students, families, and administrators.

Student Evaluation of *ReaL Book* Writing

In each *ReaL Book* Workshop, students are asked to analyze and select evidence, draft, revise, and publish writing. Along the way, students are asked to assess a student model, evaluate their own writing, and discuss their peers' writing.

Student Self-Evaluation

After students have outlined and drafted their writing, they complete a self-assessment of their writing.

Self-assessments are included in the *ReaL Book* and are based on themes and concepts addressed throughout the Workshop and the writing focus skills.

Rubrics included in the *ReaL Book* are written in student-friendly language, enabling students to easily monitor their own writing and revise their writing based on their self-assessment.

Peer-Evaluation

Once students have completed a self-assessment, they are asked to assess each other's writing. Peer-evaluation scaffolds are included in the *ReaL Book*. Students use feedback from the peer-evaluation to continue to refine their writing. Sentence frames support students' structured academic discussions.

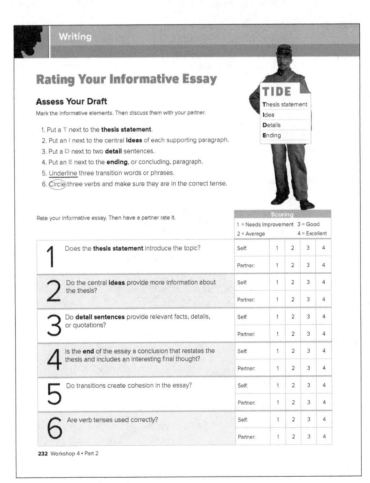

Sample Student *ReaL Book* Writing Rubric

Portfolio Assessment (continued)

Teacher Evaluation of *ReaL Book* Writing

Assess students' writing with a 4-point or 6-point rubric. Both 4-point and 6-point rubrics are available for each writing type taught in *ReaL Book*. These rubrics align directly with the strategies taught and applied during the *ReaL Book* Workshop. Student-friendly language enables you to conference with students about their individual writing results.

Student Name: _____ Date: _____

Workshop 4: Informative Essay Rubric

Use this rubric to assess student writing. Record the appropriate score in the Score column.

Criteria	Needs Improvement 1	Average 2	Good 3	Excellent 4	Score
1. A **thesis statement** states the topic and expresses a point.	Needs to identify the topic and express a point	Attempts to identify the topic and express a point	States the topic of the essay and a point	States the topic clearly and accurately with a compelling point	
2. **Central ideas** provide more information about the thesis.	Includes a few central ideas that support the thesis	Includes some central ideas that support the thesis	Includes many central ideas clearly support the thesis	Consistently uses central ideas to enhance the point made in the thesis statement	
3. **Detail sentences** provide relevant facts, details, or quotations.	Needs facts, details, or quotations, or details do not support the thesis	Includes some facts, details, and quotations, but not all connect to the thesis	Includes relevant facts, details, and quotations that connect to the thesis	Includes several relevant facts, details, and quotations that effectively connect to the thesis	
4. An **ending**, or **conclusion**, restates the thesis and includes a final thought.	Needs a conclusion, or the conclusion is abrupt or unrelated	Includes a conclusion that restates the thesis but does not provide an interesting final thought	Includes a logical conclusion that restates the thesis and provides a final thought	Develops a conclusion that restates the thesis and provides an interesting final thought	
5. **Transition words and phrases** create cohesion in the essay.	Needs transition words or phrases to create cohesion, or transitions are used incorrectly	Includes a few transition words and phrases but some may not be effective	Includes some transition words and phrases to link details	Uses varied and effective transition words and phrases to link details	
6. Correct **verb tense** is used throughout the essay.	Includes shifts in verb tense that cause confusion	Includes some shifts in verb tense that do not hinder comprehension	Includes very few shifts in verb tense	Includes no shifts in verb tense, or when shifts occur, they are logical and intentional	
7. Writing follows the **conventions** of mechanics, usage, and spelling.	Includes many errors in grammar, spelling, and punctuation that interfere with understanding	Includes some errors in grammar, spelling, and punctuation	Includes few errors in grammar, spelling, and punctuation	Uses correct grammar, spelling, and punctuation	
				Overall Score	

READ180 Universal I Stage B I Workshop 4 I Assessment I **Rubric**   Page 1 of 2

© Houghton Mifflin Harcourt Publishing Company

R180U_B_PETE_Rub_W4_InformSci4_TR

Sample 4-Point Writing Rubric

1. Select a 4-point or 6-point rubric.

2. Download the appropriate rubric from **Resources** on HMH Teacher Central and use criteria to assess each student's writing.

3. Use the accompanying Scoring Chart to assign a score for each criteria included in the rubric.

4. Determine an overall grade for the writing by averaging scores for each criteria or weighting criteria according to your own scale.

5. Share rubric assessment results with students to help them understand their writing strengths and challenges.

6. Provide time for writing revision during Checkpoints.

Assessing the *ReaL Book* Career Focus Project

Near the end of each *ReaL Book* Workshop, students are asked to complete a Career Focus Project. These projects are performance-based assessments that focus on important skills such as collaboration, supporting an argument, and synthesizing information and are tied to exciting careers. The Stage B *ReaL Book* includes:

Workshop	Career Focus	Project
1	Social Worker	Creating a Flyer
2	Water Resources Specialist	Creating a Poster
3	Publicist	Writing a Press Release
4	Journalist	Writing a News Summary
5	Epidemiologist	Tweeting Outbreak Updates
6	Personal Trainer	Writing a Blog Post

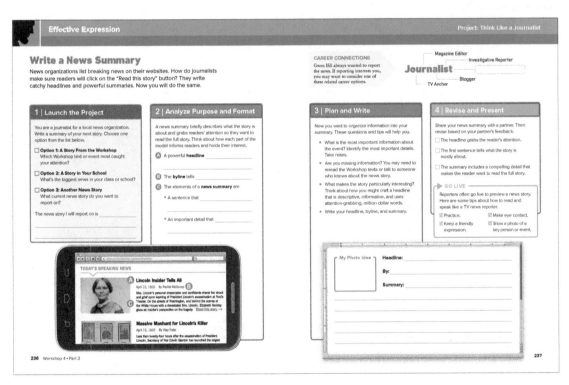

Sample Career Focus Project

Using Performance-Based Assessments

Use *ReaL Book* Career Focus Projects to assess students' learning.

- Projects require students to synthesize data from multiple *ReaL Book* readings.
- Students practice working independently, in pairs, and in groups.
- Projects help students reflect on and extend their Workshop learning. Once students have completed their *ReaL Book* Career Focus Project, use the Workshop Rubric to assess their work. (See **page 96**.)

Portfolio Assessment (continued)

Assessing *ReaL Book* Workshops

Every day, students complete work in the *ReaL Book* during Whole- and Small-Group Learning. It is important to regularly assess work and provide time to share feedback and allow time for students to revise their work.

ReaL Book Workshop Rubric

Go to **Resources** in HMH Teacher Central to access a rubric to assess comprehensive student performance in each *ReaL Book* Workshop. The rubric will allow you to review each component of the Workshop to determine student ability to respond to each task.

Name: _____   Date: _____

Workshop Rubric

Complete this rubric for each *ReaL Book* Workshop to monitor student work.

Scoring Guide
1 = Needs Improvement
2 = Average
3 = Good
4 = Excellent

Building Knowledge				
Viewing With a Purpose: Content-area words and phrases are added to the outline correctly.	1	2	3	4
Discussing Media: Responses are thoughtful. Discussion notes are recorded. A reflection is provided.				
Concept Map/Concept Organizer: Complete responses are provided for all parts of the map and organizer.				
Content-Area Vocabulary: Word knowledge is rated, definition is accurate, and example sentences are accurate and complete.				

Making Meaning				
Academic Vocabulary: Words are defined correctly. Example sentences are accurate and complete.				
Key Idea: All responses are accurate and complete.				
Comprehension Strategy: All responses are accurate and complete.				
Text Marking: Reading passages are marked (underlined, starred, boxed, checked, numbered) appropriately.				
React and Write/Stretch: Responses are thoughtful, use complete sentences, and accurately respond to the question.				
Comprehension/Literary Elements: Charts, organizers, and responses are accurate and complete.				

Language Development				
Daily Do Now: Responses are complete and include relevant content, correct word form, and correct grammar.				
Word Analysis: Charts, organizers, and responses are accurate and complete.				

READ180 Universal | Stage B | Assessment | Rubric

Name: _____   Date: _____

Workshop Rubric, continued

Writing				
Paragraph Writing: Plan, organize, and write sections are complete.	1	2	3	4
Student Model Essay: Text marking and evaluation are accurate and complete.	1	2	3	4
Plan: Organizers and responses are complete and thoughtful and include necessary elements of the writing type.	1	2	3	4
Writing Focus: Text marking and evaluation are accurate and complete. Sentence frames are accurate and complete.	1	2	3	4
Organize: Activities are completed thoughtfully using relevant text details.	1	2	3	4
Write: The response is complete.	1	2	3	4
Transitions/Conventions: Activities are completed accurately.	1	2	3	4
Self-Assessment: Peer and self-assessment feedback are complete.	1	2	3	4
Revise: Writing is revised and edited before it is published.	1	2	3	4

Career Focus Project				
Academic Vocabulary: Words are defined correctly. Example sentences are accurate and complete.	1	2	3	4
Key Idea: All responses are accurate and complete.	1	2	3	4
Comprehension Strategy: All responses are accurate and complete.	1	2	3	4

Total Workshop Score _____

Workshop Assessments and Essay	
Interim Assessment: Questions are answered accurately.	_____ / 15
End of Workshop Assessment: Questions are answered accurately.	_____ / 30
End of Workshop Constructed Response: The response uses complete sentence(s) and provides a complete and accurate response.	response 1 _____ / 2 response 2 _____ / 2
End of Workshop Writing Prompt: The response follows the rubric criteria.	_____ /
Workshop Essay: The response follows the rubric criteria.	_____ /

READ180 Universal | Stage B | Assessment | Rubric   Page 2 of 2

Completing a *ReaL Book* Workshop Rubric

Complete each section of the Workshop Rubric as students complete that portion of the Workshop, or wait until students have fully completed the Workshop before completing the rubric assessment.

Evaluate student *ReaL Book* work based on completion, accuracy, and level of complexity of student response. Consider the student's current reading level, previous Workshop work, and other external factors when determining student scores.

Score each component of the *ReaL Book* Workshop on a 1–4 scale:

ReaL Book Workshop Scoring Guide

Score	Rating	Assign when . . .
4	Excellent	Students fully and accurately complete the task.
3	Good	Students fully complete the task, but results may not be completely accurate.
2	Average	Students partially complete the task and results may be inaccurate.
1	Needs Improvement	Students do not complete the task.

Sharing Rubric Results With Students

Once you have assessed student *ReaL Book* work with the Workshop Rubric, share the rubric results with students. Students may also use the rubric to complete a self-evaluation of their work, then compare their self-assessment results with your completed rubric.

Provide an opportunity for students to discuss their *ReaL Book* progress, explain challenges, and celebrate successes. When possible, allow an opportunity for students to revise *ReaL Book* work.

ReaL Book Revision Tips

1. Circle one or two portions of the *ReaL Book* Workshop for students to revise.

2. Allow students to revise *ReaL Book* Workshop work during Whole-Group or Small-Group Learning.

3. Have students complete *ReaL Book* revision work on separate paper, and attach the paper to the original *ReaL Book* work so that you and the student can review the revisions. In this way, students are afforded an opportunity to identify and correct mistakes.

Interim and End-of-Workshop Assessments

What Workshop Assessments Measure

Assessments for each of the six Workshops in *READ 180* Universal measure knowledge transfer gained from the Workshop reading, writing, and discussion activities. Workshop Assessments also help students develop and strengthen their test-taking skills. *READ 180* Universal Workshop Assessments:

- Are aligned to core Reading and Language Arts Common Core State Standards
- Include passages at two levels of text complexity
- Provide data to inform Whole- and Small-Group Instruction
- Are structured to gradually incorporate technology-enhanced, Next Generation item types to build students' confidence

Curriculum-Based Assessment

Curriculum-based assessment occurs in the context of learning and instruction. *READ 180* curriculum-based assessments consist of periodic classroom-based tests that are aligned with *READ 180 ReaL Book* curriculum and instruction. These tests ask students to demonstrate mastery of specific strategies they were taught, rather than assessing more general achievement or reading proficiency.

READ 180's curriculum-based assessment can help you to:

- Measure students' reading success within *READ 180*
- Monitor students at the middle and end of each Workshop
- Provide information on instructional effectiveness
- Reteach and reinforce using *Resources for Differentiated Instruction* lessons

Sample digital *READ 180* Workshop Assessment Item

Assessment Types

Workshop Assessments are administered at two points per Workshop:

- **Interim Workshop Assessments** are administered at the end of Workshop Part One and assess student proficiency with strategies taught in Part One. These assessments are optional.

- **End-of-Workshop Assessments** are administered at the end of Part Two of the Workshop and assess student proficiency with strategies taught in the entire Workshop. These assessments are required.

Interim Assessment	Total Points
Reading: Comprehension and Vocabulary	15
End-of-Workshop Assessment	**Total Points**
Reading: Comprehension and Vocabulary	24
Writing & Conventions	6
Constructed Response (Optional)	4
Extended Writing (Optional)	4 or 6

Name: _____   Date: _____

READ180 Workshop 4 End-of-Workshop Assessment (Level b)

DIRECTIONS: This is a reading test. Follow the directions for each part of the test, and choose the best answer to each question.

PRACTICE QUESTION A

Read the paragraph. Then answer the question.

John Wilkes Booth's successful attack on President Lincoln stunned people all across America. Many people had been rejoicing at the end of the Civil War. Their celebrations came to an abrupt end. A nation looking forward to peace was now overcome with grief. Businesses across the country closed, and flags were flown at half-mast.

Which sentence **best** describes the author's view of Lincoln's death?

A It was a tragic event that could have been avoided.

B It was a confusing event that is difficult to understand.

C It was a strange event that made people angry.

D It was a shocking event that affected the whole country.

PRACTICE QUESTION B

Draw a line from each event in the left column to the time description in the right column.

John Wilkes Booth is captured and killed.	Event 1
There is a manhunt for John Wilkes Booth.	Event 2
The Civil War ends.	Event 3
John Wilkes Booth shoots President Lincoln.	Event 4

Go on ▶

Print versions of both the Interim and End-of-Workshop Assessments can be accessed from the Assignment Board on HMH Teacher Central.

Interim and End-of-Workshop Assessments *(continued)*

Testing Level

The Workshop Assessments accommodate students at their reading levels as well as moving them to approach grade-level text. There are two forms of each test. Level a passages are written at a below grade-level Lexile range. Level b passages are written at a basic level Lexile® range. However, the end range of the Level b passages reaches the beginning of the grade-level Lexile range. Passage readability was determined using multiple measures, including the Lexile Framework, which matches students to texts at the appropriate reading level.

Test Levels a and b assess the *same skills* and have the *same item format*. However, as the table below shows, the two levels differ in Lexile range, passage length, and qualitative measures.

Leveling Criteria	Level a Test	Level b Test
Lexile range	Stage A: 250–615L Stage B: 250–785L Stage C: 250–980L	Stage A: 540–825L Stage B: 730–1005L Stage C: 850–1180L
Length	Stage A: 150–200 words Stage B: 150–300 words Stage C: 150–300 words	Stage A: 200–600 words Stage B: 300–700 words Stage C: 300–800 words
Qualitative Measures	Shorter, simpler sentences	Longer, more complex sentences and passage structure

Digital Workshop Assessment Item Types

Help prepare students for the Digital Workshop Assessments by introducing them to the various item types they will encounter. For the initial Workshops, you may want students to first take the print version of the test and then enter their answers in the digital version. This may help alleviate some test-taking anxiety as they learn to adjust to the new item types.

The Workshop Assessments contain six types of choice questions:

- Single selected-response questions
- Multiple selected-response questions
- Two-part questions
- Highlighting questions
- Matching questions
- Chart-completion questions

They also include two types of constructed-response questions:

- Constructed response
- Extended writing

Students respond to the choice questions by scrolling over their choices and clicking to select them. When students are satisfied with their answers, they click **Next** to proceed to the next question. Students may click a different choice to change their answers at any point during the test.

Students answer constructed-response questions by composing a written response in the field provided. Students may review their written work prior to submitting it; when they are satisfied with their responses, they click **Next** to move to the next question.

Teachers may choose to include or exclude constructed-response questions and choose a rubric to score these questions in the Assignment Board in HMH Teacher Central.

Responses to constructed-response questions are forwarded to the Assignment Board for teacher evaluation against the chosen rubric.

For more information on the *READ 180* Universal program settings and using HMH Teacher Central, see the *READ 180 Workshop Assessments User's Guide* at the Houghton Mifflin Harcourt Product Support site (http://hmhco.com/read180u/productsupport).

Students may also click **Log Out** at any point in the test; their work will be saved and they will continue with the test at the point they left off the next time they log in.

On the pages that follow are some sample items as they appear on the digital test.

Interim and End-of-Workshop Assessments *(continued)*

Answering Selected-Response Questions

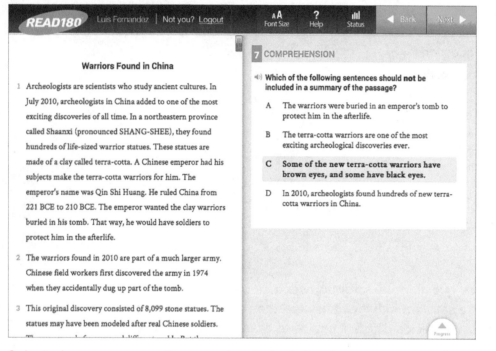

Selected-response questions require students to choose an answer from one of four choices. Workshop Assessments contain two types of selected-response questions: single and multiple. Some questions require students to choose one response; others require choosing several appropriate responses.

To answer a selected-response question, students select an answer by clicking their answer choice(s). If they are satisfied with their answers, they click **Next** to proceed to the next question. Students may click a different choice to change their answers at any point during the test.

Answering Two-Part Questions

Many questions in the Workshop Assessments have two parts. Unlike the selected-response multiple-answer questions, in which students must provide two choices to answer one question, two-part questions are broken into two individually scored parts, A and B, with each part of the question worth one point in the assessment.

To answer each part of the question, students select an answer by clicking their answer choices. If they are satisfied with their choices, they click **Next** to proceed to the next question. Students may click a different choice to change their answers at any point during the test.

Important Scoring Note: Many two-part questions ask students to identify text evidence in Part B to support their answer in Part A. If Part A is answered incorrectly, and Part B is answered correctly, no points will be given for Part B. Since the evidence in Part B is directly tied to the answer in Part A, it's clear this "correct" answer was just a guess and not a reflection of true understanding.

Interim and End-of-Workshop Assessments *(continued)*

Answering Highlighting Questions

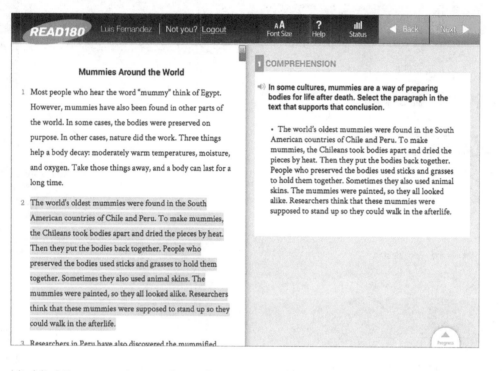

Highlighting questions ask students to answer a question by choosing a relevant sentence, section, or paragraph from a passage or excerpt.

Students answer highlighting questions by clicking their choices in the passage or excerpt. It then appears on the right side of the screen under the question. If students are satisfied with their choices, they click **Next** to go on to the next question. To change a response, they click the sentence, section, or paragraph again to deselect that response. Then, click the new response followed by clicking **Next**.

Answering Matching Questions

To make a match, students select the word or phrase on the left. Then they select its match on the right. Responses turn blue when they are selected, and a line appears linking the two columns. To change a response, click the response on the left. Then, click the response on the right. This will deselect both responses, and the line will disappear. Click the response on the left, and then click the new response on the right.

When students are satisfied with their choices, they click **Next** to go on to the next question.

Matching questions are always worth two points whether they require two or four matches. When students are making two matches, one point is given for each correct match. They must make both correct matches to receive two points. When students are making four matches, they receive zero points for one correct match, one point for two correct matches, and one point for three correct matches. They must make all four correct matches in order to receive the full two points.

Interim and End-of-Workshop Assessments (continued)

Answering Chart Questions

Students answer chart questions by clicking in a box on the chart. A blue dot appears in the chosen field. Students may click the chosen field a second time to deselect it. When students are satisfied with their choices, they click **Next** to move to the next question.

Chart completion questions are always worth two points. See example above. Where students are making two choices, one point is given for each correct choice. Students must make two correct choices to receive two points. Where students are making three choices, they receive zero points for one correct choice, one point for two correct choices, and two points for three correct choices. For questions that require four choices, students must make four correct choices in order to receive the full two points.

Sharing Results

After each Workshop Assessment, you may wish to meet with groups of students or one-on-one to discuss test results. For the print format, you can review the test answers using the completed test. For the digital Workshop Assessments, use the Student Test Printout. Be sure to grade the constructed-response and the extended writing questions using the Assignment Board on HMH Teacher Central. Writing scores entered through Assignment Board will be reflected in the Student Test Printout.

When reviewing a Workshop Assessment, you may wish to try the following strategies to help students understand their results and build confidence for future tests.

Discussing Progress

Share the overall score with a student before discussing strengths and weaknesses.

- Have students record the score in the Student Log in their *READ 180 ReaL Books*.
- Ensure that students know which questions (and strategies) they got correct and those that require more practice.
- Check the test level. If students struggled with a Level b test, remind them that it contains more difficult text and explain why you gave them the test at this level.
- Review students' previous Workshop Assessment results and discuss or preview the requirements (and level) of their next tests.

Revisiting the Test

- Identify and explain how to recognize the strategy or skill for each question.
- Encourage the student to read the question and answer choices aloud.
- Analyze each incorrect answer and encourage the student to "think aloud" about how he or she arrived at that choice.
- Have the student explain why an answer is correct or incorrect.

Reteaching Strategies

- Briefly review the skill (e.g., how to find the central idea in a passage).
- Use the *ReaL Book* to revisit how a skill was described where students first encountered it, and provide some meaningful examples.
- For comprehension questions, use a question the student answered correctly to model how an answer is supported by the passage.

Sharing Results With Parents

You may wish to share an individual student's test results with parents or caregivers. You can do this by sending a letter home or at a parent-teacher conference.

READ 180 Workshop Assessments Introduction

To learn more about the Workshop Assessments, go to **Resources** in HMH Teacher Central and download the *READ 180* Workshop Assessments Introduction.

Multimedia Performance Tasks

Interim and End-of-Year Performance Tasks

All *READ 180* Universal students complete Interim and End-of-Year Performance Tasks that take place after Workshop 3 and Workshop 6. These summative performance assessments are research projects in which students choose a topic, research and evaluate resources, and use the process and strategies they have learned for informative writing to write and present a research paper.

Teachers are provided with scaffolded lessons to ensure that students internalize the goals of the performance task and have a mental model for what their final task should look like, which will be a multimedia presentation of their research paper outcomes.

These assessments are a true barometer for showing student transfer of reading skills and comprehension to the written page and assess both their understanding of Workshop content and their ability to extend their learning.

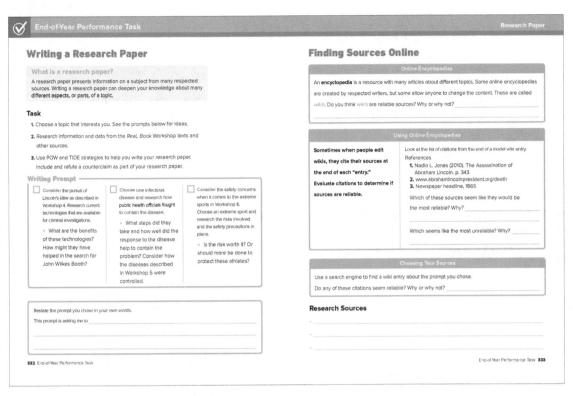

Writing a Research Paper

What is a research paper?

A research paper presents information on a subject from many respected sources. Writing a research paper can deepen your knowledge about many different aspects, or parts, of a topic.

Task

1. Choose a topic that interests you. See the prompts below for ideas.
2. Research information and data from the Real Book Workshop texts and other sources.
3. Use POW and TIDE strategies to help you write your research paper. Include and refute a counterclaim as part of your research paper.

Writing Prompt

☐ Consider the pursuit of Lincoln's killer as described in Workshop 4. Research current technologies that are available for criminal investigations.
- What are the benefits of these technologies? How might they have helped in the search for John Wilkes Booth?

☐ Choose one infectious disease and research how public health officials fought to contain the disease.
- What steps did they take and how well did the response to the disease help to contain the problem? Consider how the diseases described in Workshop 5 were controlled.

☐ Consider the safety concerns when it comes to the extreme sports in Workshop 6. Choose an extreme sport and research the risks involved and the safety precautions in place.
- Is the risk worth it? Or should more be done to protect these athletes?

Restate the prompt you chose in your own words.

This prompt is asking me to ___

Finding Sources Online

Online Encyclopedias

An **encyclopedia** is a resource with many articles about different topics. Some online encyclopedias are created by respected writers, but some allow anyone to change the content. These are called *wikis*. Do you think *wikis* are reliable sources? Why or why not? ___

Using Online Encyclopedias

Sometimes when people edit wikis, they cite their sources at the end of each "entry." Evaluate citations to determine if sources are reliable.

Look at the list of citations from the end of a model wiki entry.

References
1. Nadia L. Jones (2010). The Assassination of Abraham Lincoln. p. 343
2. www.abrahamlincolnpresident.org/death
3. Newspaper headline, 1865

Which of these sources seem like they would be the most reliable? Why? ___

Which seems like the most unreliable? Why? ___

Choosing Your Sources

Use a search engine to find a wiki entry about the prompt you chose.

Do any of these citations seem reliable? Why or why not? ___

Research Sources

- ___
- ___
- ___

Use the Performance Tasks to guide students to conduct research effectively and evaluate the reliability of various print and digital resources.

Create a Multimedia Presentation

Use your research paper to create a multimedia presentation that will help you present your research to the class. This presentation should use other media and graphics, such as images, charts, audio, or video. Choose your presentation format:

☐ Film a short video   ☐ Create a website   ☐ Choose your own format

WHY USE MULTIMEDIA

- Media can *clarify* claims and findings by showing information in a different way.
- Media can *emphasize* important points in your presentation.
- Media can *strengthen* evidence in your presentation.
- Media can *enhance* your presentation by making it more engaging and interesting.

Plan Your Presentation

- Based on my research, I created a ___, using ___
- This (image/slide/video/chart/audio clip) (is an example of/supports the idea that/is evidence that) ___
- I chose to use ___ (type of media) to present my research because ___
- I'd like to give credit to my research sources. They can be found on my works cited, which is shown ___

PRESENTATION SKILLS

- Make eye contact with your classmates.
- Speak slowly and loudly.
- Use notes, but don't read from them directly during the entire presentation.
- Practice with a classmate before presenting. Ask her or him for feedback.

Listen and Respond

While your classmates present, you will be listening closely so that you can respond with feedback and questions. Keep the following questions in mind while you listen:

☐ What is one question you have for the presenter?

Language to Report
I have a question about ___.
Can you explain why ___?

☐ What about the presentation did you find most interesting?

Language to Discuss and Compare
The information I found compelling was ___.
Like ___, I was intrigued by ___.

☐ Which presentation skill did the presenter use the most effectively?

Language to Report
I appreciated how he/she ___.
I felt engaged in the presentation because ___.

☐ How did the type of media used enhance the presentation? How could another type of media work?

Language to Report
___ supports the evidence that ___ because ___.
___ could be an appropriate way to show this evidence because ___.

Having students present their research helps to strengthen their speaking and listening skills. Support students to choose visuals that are impactful and to prepare talking points that highlight key aspects of their research topics.

Multimedia Performance Tasks (continued)

Assessing the Performance Tasks

Each Performance Task includes a writing rubric to assess the qualities of a thoroughly researched essay as well as a presentation rubric to assess how well students were able to present their findings using multimedia.

Student Name: _____   Date: _____

End-of-Year Performance Task: Research Paper

Use this rubric to assess student writing. Record the appropriate score in the Score column.

Criteria	Needs Improvement 1	Average 2	Good 3	Excellent 4	Score
1. A **thesis statement** states the topic and expresses a point.	Needs to identify the topic and express a point	Attempts to identify the topic and express a point	States the topic of the essay and a point	States the topic clearly and accurately with a compelling point	
2. **Central ideas** provide more information about the thesis.	Includes a few central ideas that support the thesis	Includes some central ideas that support the thesis	Includes many ideas that clearly support the thesis	Consistently uses central ideas to enhance the point made in the thesis statement	
3. **Detail sentences** provide evidence, like facts, details, or quotations from research sources.	Needs evidence from research sources to support the thesis	Includes some evidence from research sources, but not all evidence connects to the thesis	Includes relevant evidence from research sources that connect to the thesis	Includes several relevant types of evidence from **sources that effectively** connect to the thesis	
4. A **conclusion** restates the thesis and includes a final thought.	Needs a conclusion, or the conclusion is abrupt or unrelated	Includes a conclusion that restates the thesis but does not provide an interesting final thought	Includes a logical conclusion that restates the thesis and provides a final thought	Develops a conclusion that restates the thesis and provides an interesting final thought	
5. **In-text citations** are used correctly in paper to cite research sources.	Needs to include in-text citations to give credit to research sources	Includes a few in-text citations, but the format may not be correct	Includes some in-text citations, but not every time evidence is used from a research source	Includes many in-text citations and citations are formatted correctly	
6. Writing follows **conventions** of mechanics, usage, and spelling.	Includes many errors in grammar, spelling, and punctuation that interfere with understanding	Includes some errors in grammar, spelling, and punctuation	Includes few errors in grammar, spelling, and punctuation	Uses correct grammar, spelling, and punctuation	
7. A **works cited** is included, which provides more information about the research sources used.	Needs a works cited to give more information about research sources used	Includes a works cited, but is not in the correct format, or it does not provide all the information	Includes a works cited that lists all research sources with a few errors in format	Includes a works cited that lists all research sources, and provides all information in the correct format	
				Overall Score	

READ180 Universal | Stage B | ReaL Book | Performance Task | **Rubric**   Page 1 of 2

© Houghton Mifflin Harcourt Publishing Company

R180U_B_PETE_Rub_EOYResPap4_TR

To access the End-of-Year Performance Task Writing Rubric, go to Resources in HMH Teacher Central.

Student Name: _____ Date: _____

End-of-Year Performance Task: Multimedia Presentation

Use this rubric to assess student presentations. Record the appropriate score in the Score column.

Criteria	Needs Improvement 1	Average 2	Good 3	Excellent 4	Score
1. The student follows instructions **to plan the presentation based on the research paper.**	Needs to include elements of research paper, for example evidence from sources, a counterclaim, a works cited, etc.	Attempts to base presentation on research paper, but does not give credit to research sources or does not include a counterclaim.	Bases presentation on research paper, including some evidence from research sources, a works cited, and a counterclaim.	Bases presentation on research paper, includes and refutes a counterclaim, consistently uses evidence, and includes a bibliography.	
2. The student **includes multimedia elements (images, charts, audio, video)** in presentation.	Needs to include multimedia elements in presentation	Includes a few multimedia elements, but does not base the presentation around them	Includes some multimedia elements, working them into the topic of the presentation	Includes many multimedia elements, effectively basing the presentation around them	
3. The student effectively **uses multimedia to enhance the presentation.**	Uses multimedia, but it is irrelevant or redundant	Uses multimedia, but it does not effectively enhance the presentation	Uses some multimedia to enhance presentation, but some is redundant or irrelevant	Uses many multimedia elements that enhance the claims and evidence in the presentation	
4. The student follows instructions on **presentation skills** (making eye contact with classmates, speaking slowly and loudly, pronunciation, etc.).	Needs to make eye contact, speak slowly and loudly, ask about pronunciation of unknown words	Uses one or two presentation skills, but does not use them consistently	Makes eye contact, and speaks slowly and loudly, but not consistently. Asks about pronunciation for some but not all unknown words	Consistently makes eye contact, and speaks slowly and loudly. Asks about pronunciation for all unknown words, and pronounces them correctly	
5. The student **listens** to other presentations and **responds with comments and questions.**	Needs to respond with relevant comments and questions	Responds to questions asked directly about a presentation, but does not offer feedback or analysis	Reports on topic of presentation, and offers feedback	Reports on topic of presentation, and offers insightful feedback and analysis of presentation	
				Overall Score	

To access the End-of-Year Presentation Rubric, go to Resources in HMH Teacher Central.

READ180

Assessment & Analytics Guide

Houghton Mifflin Harcourt

Placement & Exiting

Progress Monitoring

Curricul. Embedd. Assessm.

Oral Fluency Assessment

Assessment for Learning

Data Analytics & Communication

Oral Fluency Assessment

Understand how data from the Student Application Success Zone recordings and words correct per minute scores (WCPM) from Oral Fluency Assessments (OFA) can help inform instructional decisions to best support students' fluency development.

Oral Fluency

Oral fluency is the ability to read connected text at a pace that allows comprehension of grade-level reading materials. Fluent readers decode text and recognize sight words automatically. This ability is critical to comprehension because it allows the reader to focus on meaning, rather than on decoding each word. Oral fluency assessment is one of multiple measures you can use to monitor your students' progress and inform instruction.

Oral Fluency Practice

Students must spend time reading aloud so you can gauge their progress with oral reading fluency. Regularly assess fluency levels to quickly identify students who may have a fluency problem that requires additional instructional support.

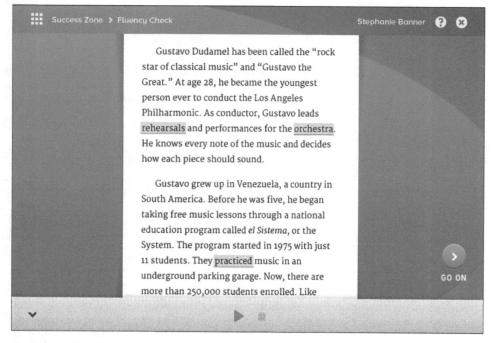

In Fluency Check, students can listen to their final recording and highlight words they missed. These words are reviewed in the future segments.

Fluency Check

The culminating activity in the Success Zone is a final recording called **Fluency Check**. It provides students with the opportunity to demonstrate mastery of the passage they have been focusing on during the current segment. Students read and make oral recordings of the passage multiple times during the Reading Zone. When students enter the Success Zone, they make a final oral recording of the passage, perform a self-assessment, re-record it if they choose, then save the recording. This activity provides students with a sense of how their reading fluency has improved.

When students complete a recording, the **Self-Check** button appears. As students listen to their recording, they may click words they missed to highlight them. Students may review their success at the end of the playback by completing the Student Self-Rating.

Assessing Oral Fluency Practice Results

Once students have completed an oral fluency recording in the Success Zone of the *READ 180* Student Application, you will be able to review it in the Assignment Board.

Grading Oral Fluency Results on the Assignment Board

To assess a student's oral fluency recording from HMH Teacher Central, follow these steps:

1. Click on the student's name in the Assignment Board in HMH Teacher Central.

2. Click on Fluency Check link. This will bring up a copy of the passage so that you can follow along while you listen to the student's recording.

3. Click **Play** to listen to the student's recording.

4. Use the **Highlight** button to mark disfluent words. Once you have listened to the recording, click the **Highlight** button again to calculate Correct Words Per Minute.

5. Use the rubric in the Assignment Board to assign a fluency score. Compare to student self-rating.

6. Click **Save**, then click **Submit**. Results will appear in the Student Application report.

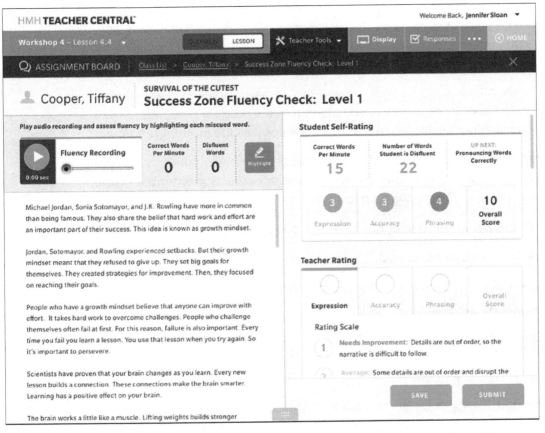

Use the Success Zone Fluency Check in the Assignment Board to rate students' final recordings.

Oral Fluency Assessment

An Oral Fluency Assessment, or OFA, measures the number of words correct per minute (WCPM) that students read. You can compare your students' WCPM score with an overall average of students' WCPM scores at their grade level to see if their fluency levels are above, below, or on grade level. This assessment involves taking one-minute samples of students' oral reading. Reading passages should include fiction and nonfiction.

When to Administer an Oral Fluency Assessment

An Oral Fluency Assessment may be administered one-on-one, three times a year. Go to **Resources** in HMH Teacher Central and search for **Assessing Oral Reading Fluency**. There you can download instructions and choose from a range of grade-level passages.

How to Administer an Oral Fluency Assessment

Follow these steps to assess a student's oral fluency.

1. Print two copies of each passage—one for the student and one for you to record errors.

2. Before the timed reading begins, say to the student, *Today you are going to take an Oral Fluency Assessment. I'm going to give you a sheet of paper with a passage written on it. You may not know all the words in the passage, but try your best to read each of them. I will tell you how to read the words you do not know. I will time you for one minute.*

3. Hand your student a copy of the passage. Tell the student, *I will begin timing as soon as you begin reading. After one minute, I will say "Stop" so you will know to stop reading.* Begin timing as soon as the student starts reading.

4. As the student reads, follow along on your copy of the passage, marking words read incorrectly with an "X" and pronouncing words aloud that the student does not know. Remember the following guidelines when marking your copy as the student reads:

   a. For a word to be read correctly, it should be read correctly in context. For example, when reading the word *live* in the following sentence, the student must pronounce it with a long-i sound: "There was a live audience."

   b. Self-corrections within three seconds are counted as correct.

   c. Repetitions are counted as correct.

   d. Consider the following as words read incorrectly:

      • **Mispronunciations**—words that are misread. For example, *ship* for *sheep*.

      • **Substitutions of any kind**—words that are substituted for the correct word. For example, *dog* for *cat*.

      • **Omissions**—words that are skipped or not read.

      • **Words that students struggle to read for three or more seconds.** When this occurs, pronounce the word for the student and have him or her continue reading. Count the word as incorrect.

5. After one minute, say *"Stop!"* Make a vertical line after the last word the student read.

OFA Miscue Analysis

Diving in Deeper: Miscue Analysis

If you want to understand the strengths and weaknesses of your students, you can take a closer look at the miscues (incorrect guesses) that they make during reading.

- Miscue analysis is a tool for assessing students' comprehension based on samples of oral reading.

- Miscues indicate if a reader is understanding and seeking meaning from the text.

- Miscue analysis gives the teacher data about the learner's reading strategies. Students' mistakes are usually not random, but actually their attempt to make sense of the text with their experiences and skills.

Scoring System

Errors can be recorded in different ways, but the chart below includes the most useful. It may be helpful to digitally record a student during a miscue analysis. Since it is difficult to carry out a running analysis, the ability to replay the recording and hear the errors again is essential for accurate marking.

Miscue	Symbol	
Non-Response	work	Use a broken line to indicate an inability or refusal to attempt a word.
Substitution	Play / work	Write the substituted word above the appropriate part of the text.
		If a learner uses a nonword, record it reflecting the grapho/phonic cues being used; e.g., phenomena *pronounced as* fu-hon-ma *should be written as* phuhonma, *showing their knowledge of* ph.
Insertion	his / for work	Indicate by using an insertion sign and writing the word above.
Omission	(work)	Circle the word, words, or parts of words missing.
Repetition	work	Underline the words repeated.
Correction	play © / work	Place a small *c* beside the corrected word. Place an *mc* for miscorrection.
Reversal	work hard / o n	Symbol that shows which part of letters, words, phrases, or clauses have been interchanged.
Hesitation	work/hard / work//hard	One slash indicates hesitation between two words. Two slashes indicate extra-long hesitation.

"Scoring System Chart" adapted from "Miscue Analysis" by M. Walsh (June 1979) from the LSIS website. Copyright © Learning and Skills Improvement Service. Used by permission.

Interpreting Oral Fluency Results

After a student has read the passage aloud, follow these steps to calculate words correct per minute (WCPM).

1. Count the total number of words read in each passage.

2. Count the total number of words read incorrectly in each passage, and subtract that number from the total number of words read. This will give you the WCPM score. For each student, you will need three WCPMs to produce a meaningful score.

3. Once you have three scores, take the median, or middle, score. For example, a student who scores 98, 101, and 104, has a median WCPM of 101.

4. Compare the student's median score to the Oral Reading Fluency Norms chart on the next page to determine whether the student is reading above, on, or below grade level.

5. Record the student's score.

Understanding Oral Reading Fluency Norms

The Oral Reading Fluency Norms chart on **page 119** contains research-based oral fluency benchmarks that are good indicators of overall reading proficiency. Use these norms to measure students' fluency against standards for their grade and the time of year.

Follow these steps to determine whether a student's fluency is above, on, or below grade level:

1. Find the student's grade level on the Oral Reading Fluency Norms chart. Then look at the time of year during which testing took place.

2. Compare the student's median WCPM (the median score from the three passages read aloud) with the numbers shown for that grade level and time of year. Note where the student's WCPM falls in the Percentile column.

   - 90th Percentile: Significantly above grade level
   - 75th Percentile: Above grade level
   - 50th Percentile: Grade level
   - 25th Percentile: Below grade level
   - 10th Percentile: Far below grade level

Using Results to Set Fluency Goals

Set a few measureable goals that can be achieved using intervention strategies: repeated readings, phrase-cueing texts, speed drills, and periodic monitoring. Go to **Resources** in HMH Teacher Central and search for **Fluency Routines**.

Oral Reading Fluency Norms

This chart displays the norms for Oral Reading Fluency. The norms are updated at the fall, winter, and spring of each year. These norms are from the *2006 Hasbrouck & Tindal Oral Reading Fluency Data*.

Grade	Percentile	Fall WCPM*	Winter WCPM*	Spring WCPM*	Avg. Weekly Improvement**
1	90		81	111	1.9
	75		47	82	2.2
	50		23	53	1.9
	25		12	28	1.0
	10		6	15	0.6
2	90	106	125	142	1.1
	75	79	100	117	1.2
	50	51	72	89	1.2
	25	25	42	61	1.1
	10	11	18	31	0.6
3	90	128	146	162	1.1
	75	99	120	137	1.2
	50	71	92	107	1.1
	25	44	62	78	1.1
	10	21	36	48	0.8
4	90	145	166	180	1.1
	75	119	139	152	1.0
	50	94	112	123	0.9
	25	68	87	98	0.9
	10	45	61	72	0.8
5	90	166	182	194	0.9
	75	139	156	168	0.9
	50	110	127	139	0.9
	25	85	99	109	0.8
	10	61	74	83	0.7
6	90	177	195	204	0.8
	75	153	167	177	0.8
	50	127	140	150	0.7
	25	98	111	122	0.8
	10	68	82	93	0.8
7	90	180	192	202	0.7
	75	156	165	177	0.7
	50	128	136	150	0.7
	25	102	109	123	0.7
	10	79	88	98	0.6
8	90	185	199	199	0.4
	75	161	173	177	0.5
	50	133	146	151	0.6
	25	106	115	124	0.6
	10	77	84	97	0.6

* WCPM = Words Correct Per Minute ** Average words-per-week growth

Data-Driven Instructional Decision Making

Discover how to use dynamic grouping tools to facilitate classroom management. Maximize the benefits from the real-time performance data they collect to digitally diagnose learning needs to provide targeted differentiated instruction.

Adjusting Groups and Instruction

Differentiating Instruction in *READ 180*

READ 180 supports differentiated instruction that targets individual student needs in all rotations. HMH *Reading Inventory* results are used to place students into appropriate Student App levels, select Independent Reading texts, group students, and adjust instruction to support varying student needs.

Differentiating Instruction With the Student Application

The *READ 180* Student Application is "intelligent software" that collects data from students' individual responses, continuously assessing each student's progress and adjusting instruction accordingly. It is organized into 25 segments, each containing a consistent set of activities that build essential knowledge in an engaging, age-appropriate topic. Within a segment, students complete activities in six instructional zones.

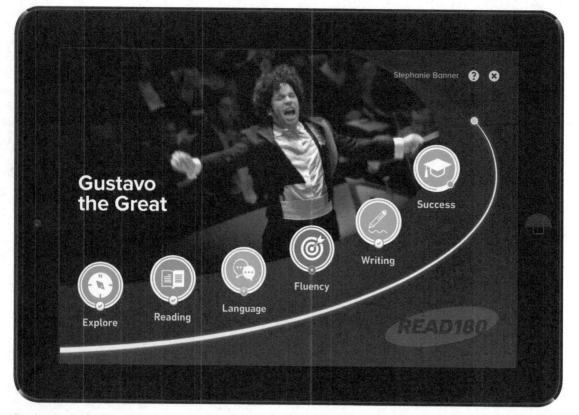

Beginning in the Explore Zone and ending in the Success Zone, students follow a personalized path that accelerates their learning.

The Student Application Zone Overview

Zone	Description	Support Options
EXPLORE ZONE • Build Background & Concept Knowledge	Students develop academic language with Anchor Videos that build background knowledge and strengthen vocabulary.	• Download the Segment Overview and use the Anchor Video Summary to pre-teach key concepts.
READING ZONE • Build Deep Comprehension Through Close Reading	Individualized texts and comprehension tasks offer students adaptive practice with Next Generation item types based on the Depth of Knowledge (DOK) framework.	• Listen to students' recordings to assess their fluency performance on initial readings. • Identify strategies and/or DOK levels student is struggling with. • Identify possible inconsistencies between student self-ratings and their performance.
LANGUAGE ZONE • Develop Robust Academic Vocabulary and Language	These language-based activities help students build and expand their academic vocabulary and confidence.	• Download the Segment Overview, and pre-teach Power Words students will encounter in their current segment. • Re-teach vocabulary words with low scores.
FLUENCY ZONE • Decode and Encode With Fluency and Automaticity	Students practice spelling and reading sight words to build automaticity, which allows their cognitive resources to focus on comprehension and retention.	• Identify and teach decoding and spelling patterns with low scores.
WRITING ZONE • Systematic Writing Instruction to Facilitate Effective Expression	Students experience each stage of the writing process as they plan, organize, write, and publish argumentative, narrative, and informative essays for each segment topic.	• Use the Assignment Board writing rubric results to identify whether students are fully engaging in the writing process. • Look for inconsistencies between student self-ratings and their performance.
SUCCESS ZONE • Apply Learning to Grade-Level Text	Students build and apply the fluency and comprehension strategies they have learned and practiced in the other zones to demonstrate comprehension and keep progressing forward.	• Use the Assignment Board Fluency Check to evaluate students' final recordings to assess fluency gains. • Ensure students are showing high levels of comprehension.

Adjusting Groups and Instruction (continued)

The Student Application Activity Flowchart

The research-based instructional sequence offers students continuous support and immediate feedback. This feedback is nonjudgmental, private, and encouraging, allowing students to practice at the level they need without embarrassment.

EXPLORE ZONE
- Anchor Video
- Knowledge for Reading

READING ZONE: MODELED READ
- Read / Record
- Rate
- Comprehension Tasks (2)

READING ZONE: CLOSE READ

STRATEGY 1	STRATEGY 2	STRATEGY 3
Read / Record	Read	Read
Rate	Rate	Rate
Comprehension Tasks 3+1	Comprehension Tasks 3+1	Comprehension Tasks 3+1

STUDENT CHOICE

LANGUAGE ZONE

WORD CARDS
- Words in Context
- Word Family
- Synonyms & Antonyms
- Examples & Non-Examples

FLUENCY ZONE

SPELLING	WORD
Spelling Assessment	Word Assessment
Spelling Clinic	Word Clinic
Spelling Challenge	Word Match
Proofreading	Self-Check
	Speed Challenge

WRITING ZONE
- Plan
- Write
- Revise & Edit
- Publish

SUCCESS ZONE

LEVELS 1-3	LEVELS 4-6
Discrepancy Task	Discrepancy Task
Context Task	Fluency Check
Fluency Check	Stretch Read
	Read
	Rate
	Comprehension Tasks (2)

Activities within each zone collect data from students' individual responses, continuously assessing each student's progress and adjusting instruction accordingly.

Automatic Student App Leveling

The *READ 180* Student Application uses students' initial *Reading Inventory* results to place each student at the appropriate level.* *Reading Inventory* scores do not affect a student's level after the initial placement in the Student Application. Students are promoted in *READ 180* based on performance in each zone.

Manually Adjusting Student App Levels

At times, you may wish to adjust a student's *READ 180* level based on your observations. Use data from *READ 180* Student Application reports and the student's classroom performance to determine appropriate student levels.*

When manually adjusting Student Application levels, the level promotion will not take effect until the student begins the next segment. Once a student is promoted to a new level, the student will have access to all segments at the new level.

	Automatic Leveling Occurs...	**Choose to Manually Adjust Leveling...**

Leveling Up	• If student scores are above this criteria in two consecutive segments:
	    90% on Close Read items
	    95% on Word Assessment items
	    90% on Spelling Assessment items
		• If a student does not accept the Student App level-up challenge, conference with them to determine why. (Note: The Student App will level up at the start of their next segment.)
		• Consider leveling up when a midyear *Reading Inventory* score is above a student's current level range.
		• If student scores are consistently high for more than two segments and near criteria for automatic level up.

Leveling Down	Students are not automatically leveled down in the Student App.	• If student scores are below this criteria in two consecutive segments:
		    60% on Close Read items
		    80% on Word Assessment items
		    70% on Spelling Assessment items
		• If a student appears to be disengaged during Student App use, conference with them and determine if the difficulty of activities is a factor.

*Lexile range for each *READ 180* Level

READ 180 Level	Stage A Elementary	Stage B Middle School	Stage C High School
Level 1	450–600L	450–600L	450–600L
Level 2	550–700L	550–700L	550–700L
Level 3	650–800L	650–800L	650–800L
Level 4	750–900L	750–900L	750–900L
Level 5	850–1050L	850–1050L	850–1050L
Level 6	N/A	1000–1200L	1000–1300L+

Differentiating Instruction With Independent Reading

In addition to placing students appropriately in the *READ 180* Student Application, *Reading Inventory* results are used to match readers with appropriate texts in Independent Reading.

The *READ 180* Independent Reading Library contains multiple books at each *READ 180* level, written to appropriate levels of readability. These titles span a wide range of genres to appeal to a variety of readers.

Tailor the Independent Reading rotation to meet individual student needs by assisting students in selecting books, eBooks, and eReads at their reading level and interest. Then, vary the level of scaffolding and support you provide based on the text complexity. For example, provide more opportunities for book conferences and completion of written scaffolding such as graphic organizers and QuickWrites when students are reading more complex texts.

Results from The *Reading Inventory* help students select books at their appropriate reading level.

Differentiating Small-Group Learning

The Advantages of Learning in Small Groups

Grouping and regrouping students for targeted instruction maximizes teachers' effectiveness. During Small-Group Learning, *READ 180* students will:

- Have more opportunities to participate
- Benefit from immediate, corrective feedback
- Gain confidence in sharing ideas
- Build upon one another's strengths
- Become more self-directed learners by setting and attaining individual goals

Grouping for Daily *ReaL Book* Instruction

Effective differentiated instruction is based on student performance results. *READ 180* provides support and scaffolding for dynamic and flexible grouping to allow for differentiated instruction within each *ReaL Book* Workshop.

The *ReaL Book* provides comprehensive daily reading, vocabulary, and writing instruction. Groups for daily *ReaL Book* instruction are based on common areas of instructional focus, which allows for targeted instruction to address specific areas of need.

Using the Groupinator™ to Manage Groups

The Groupinator streamlines the process of differentiating instruction and regrouping students. This essential *READ 180* tool allows you to view student data and organize students into groups based on categories such as Lexile measure and reading strategy performance.

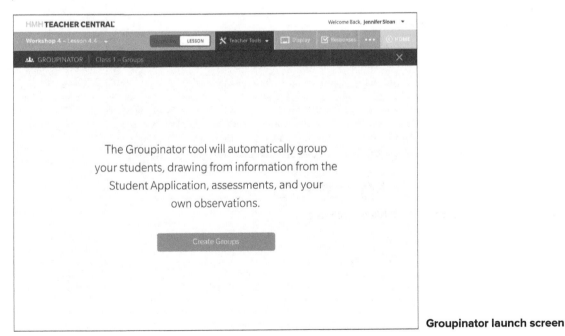

Groupinator launch screen

Differentiating Small-Group Learning (continued)

When to Run the Groupinator

Consider using the Groupinator to regroup students:

- During the Getting Started section of the *ReaL Book* to form initial groups
- After completing Part 1 of a Workshop (Interim Checkpoint)
- After completing Part 2 of a Workshop (End-of-Workshop Checkpoint)
- After students complete a *Reading Inventory* assessment
- At the beginning of a *ReaL Book* Workshop
- According to school calendar milestones

For the *Digital Teacher's Edition*, use the Table of Content to track when you have completed Part 1 or Part 2 of a Workshop. For best results, administer the *READ 180* Workshop Assessment before you run the Groupinator. For Part 1, the Interim test assesses strategies taught in Part 1 of a Workshop.

Sample *ReaL Book Digital Teacher's Edition* Part 1 Table of Contents

WORKSHOP 4 PREVIEW
The Hunt for Lincoln's Killer

Use this overview of lesson texts and types to preview the teaching and learning for this Workshop.

WHAT'S SIGNIFICANT ABOUT *The Hunt for Lincoln's Killer?*
President Lincoln's assassination by John Wilkes Booth on April 14, 1865, shocked the nation. The murder set off a 12-day manhunt for the killer. More importantly, the event itself—as well as the reactions of Americans who both admired and criticized Lincoln—crystalized the conflicts that had caused Northern and Southern states to fight each other in the Civil War for four long and bloody years.

HMH **TEACHER CENTRAL**

Download these resources for planning information, including Standards-Based Lesson Goals, Resources for Differentiated Instruction, and detailed text information.
• Workshop 4 Planning Guide
• Workshop 4 Text Overview
• Daily Lesson Plans

KEY TO THE COLORS
Building Knowledge
Making Meaning
Language Development
Writing
Effective Expression

PART 1

LESSON 4.1 Workshop Opener and Anchor Video
Preview the Workshop. Build background via the Anchor Video.

LESSON 4.2 Concept Map & Content-Area Vocabulary
Connect to the Key Concept: conflict
Frontload content-area vocabulary.

LESSON 4.3 Who Was John Wilkes Booth?
Students find out John Wilkes Booth's background and his motives for wanting to assassinate President Lincoln.

LESSON 4.4–4.5 from Chasing Lincoln's Killer
This excerpt from James L. Swanson's award-winning book Chasing Lincoln's Killer transports students to Ford's Theater on the day that President Lincoln was shot.

LESSON 4.6 Build Comprehension
Deepen Text Comprehension: People, Events, and Ideas.

LESSON 4.7 Language Development
• Morphology Focus: Suffixes –able, –ible
• Vocabulary Strategy: Denotation and Connotation

LESSONS 4.8–4.9 from Behind the Scenes
Students read a first-hand account of the aftermath of President Lincoln's assassination from the perspective of a former slave who became a White House confidant.

LESSON 4.10 Build Comprehension
Deepen Text Comprehension: Author's Point of View

LESSON 4.11 Paragraph Writing
Writing a Paragraph: Analyze how people in Washington, DC, reacted to President Lincoln's assassination in Behind the Scenes.

INTERIM WORKSHOP ASSESSMENT
LESSON 4.12 CHECKPOINT

PART 2

LESSON 4.13 Concept Organizer & Content-Area Vocabulary
Connect to the Key Concept: respect
Frontload content-area vocabulary.

OPTIONAL Digital-Only Fluency Text
"Presidential Protectors" explains the origin and purpose of the Secret Service.

LESSON 4.14–4.15 Tracking an Assassin
This time line leaders on a thrilling 12-day-long manhunt for assassin John Wilkes Booth.

LESSON 4.16 A Nation Mourns
Students trace the path of Lincoln's funeral train as Americans pay tribute to their fallen president.

LESSON 4.17 O Captain! My Captain!
Students encounter Walt Whitman's poetic tribute to the president he deeply admired.

LESSON 4.18 Build Comprehension
Analyze Literary Elements: Extended Metaphor

LESSON 4.19 Essay Writing
Analyze a model informative essay.

LESSON 4.20 Essay Writing
Plan Your Essay: Identify two people in this Workshop who reacted strongly to President Lincoln's assassination.

LESSON 4.21 Essay Writing
Writing Focus: Introductions
Organize and draft essay.

LESSON 4.22 Essay Writing
Transitions and Conventions
• Create Cohesion
• Using Correct Verb Tense

LESSON 4.23 Essay Writing
Assess: Rating Your Informative Essay

LESSON 4.24 Career Focus & Project
• Career Focus: Reporting From Washington
• Project: Write a News Summary

END-OF-WORKSHOP ASSESSMENT
LESSON 4.25 CHECKPOINT

T188   *READ 180* UNIVERSAL Blended Learning Handbook

Workshop 4 Preview   T189

Sample *Blended Learning Handbook* Workshop Preview

For the *Blended Learning Handbook*, use the Workshop Preview to track completion of Part 1 or Part 2 of a Workshop. For best results, administer the *READ 180* End-of-Workshop Assessment *before* you run the Groupinator. This test assesses strategies taught in both Part 1 and Part 2 of a Workshop and the data will help inform the algorithm.

Differentiating Small-Group Learning (continued)

How to Use the Groupinator

Follow these simple steps to group students for differentiated instruction based on relevant performance data.

STEP 1

Go to Teacher Tools

In HMH Teacher Central, access the Groupinator from the Teacher Tool pull-down menu.

STEP 2

Choose Number of Groups

Select the number of groups that matches your blended learning model. Most *READ 180* classrooms use three groups, but your classroom's grouping may vary depending on block scheduling and other considerations.

STEP 3

Choose Your Groups' Focus

The Groupinator suggests groups based on data synthesized from *The Reading Inventory*, *READ 180* Workshop Assessments, the Student App, and teacher-entered formative assessment information.

Choose to group students by one of five criteria:

- Reading Comprehension
- Language & Vocabulary
- Lexile Measure
- Writing
- Word Study

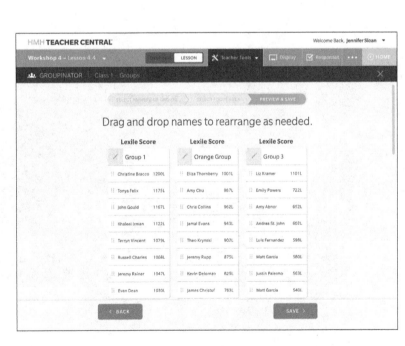

STEP 4

Review and Personalize Results

Customize groups based on your own observations of students' behavior and academic performance.

Assessment for Learning

Self-assessment encourages students to actively participate in the learning process and invest in the outcome of their work. Learn how to implement self-assessment strategies to establish a collaborative classroom culture.

Developing Student Self-Assessment

What Is Self-Assessment?

Self-assessment is the process by which a student generates internal feedback. The student sets a goal, strategizes how to achieve that goal, works toward the goal, and then evaluates how far toward the goal he or she has gotten over the course of an assignment or a series of assignments. (*For more information on self-assessment as a formative assessment and how to conduct self-assessments using the* ReaL Book, *see pages* **88-91.***)*

When done correctly, students are able to use self-assessment to coordinate their existing knowledge with their emotions and actions to meet new learning goals. Self-assessment allows students to become aware of their strengths and weaknesses, and develop learning tools and strategies tailored to their needs. This process emphasizes developing skills that can be applied to new situations rather than just the act of earning a grade or reward.

Why Teach Self-Assessment

Self-assessment focuses on developing skills that have many applications, both in and out of the classroom. One fundamental skill self-assessment develops is self-awareness. During the process of self-assessment, students constantly evaluate their understanding of what they learn, what challenges they face, what they've accomplished, and what they still need to improve on. This helps them become aware of their strengths and weaknesses.

Self-assessment focuses not only on evaluation of past work, but also on prediction of future outcomes. Students set goals for themselves before they begin working on a task. By examining the goals students set for themselves and the thought processes, successes, and challenges they meet along the way to achieving those goals, students develop critical thinking skills. Critical thinking skills are crucial for them to determine for themselves which learning strategies are most effective to meet their learning needs.

Over time, students will also develop self-efficacy, or the ability to project their likelihood of success in pursuit of a proposed goal, and adjust accordingly with relation to time and strategy. The more they hone their strategy and achieve success with goals they have set, the more students perceive themselves as motivated, successful, and competent.

Self-Assessment in the Classroom

Successful self-assessment is made up of many small steps. Initially, you should create structure and scaffold every step in the cycle; but over time, students will internalize the process of evaluating themselves and will need less guidance to self-regulate. Evaluating student progress should be an ongoing process, and each step in the cycle can be repeated as many times as is helpful.

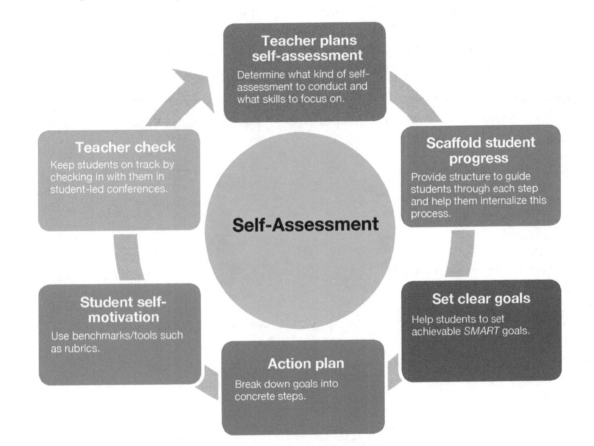

Teacher plans self-assessment
Determine what kind of self-assessment to conduct and what skills to focus on.

Scaffold student progress
Provide structure to guide students through each step and help them internalize this process.

Set clear goals
Help students to set achievable *SMART* goals.

Action plan
Break down goals into concrete steps.

Student self-motivation
Use benchmarks/tools such as rubrics.

Teacher check
Keep students on track by checking in with them in student-led conferences.

Self-Assessment

Follow these steps to establish a self-assessment protocol in the classroom.

How to Teach Self-Assessment

The key elements to successful self-assessment are frequent practice, clear goal setting, strategic planning, and evaluation of progress. There are several techniques and tools you can employ to teach effective self-assessment. One technique is to help students set goals that are manageable and clear. Each large goal should be broken down into small, concrete steps so that a student's progress can be measured. Other effective techniques include using rubrics to provide clear criteria for students to use in evaluating themselves and setting up student-led conferencing.

Developing Student Self-Assessment *(continued)*

Scaffolding Student Progress

The eventual goal of self-assessment is for students to be able to process their own experiences and internalize strategies to help them learn. Provide goals and strategies to students when you introduce the idea of self-assessment. Conducting student-led conferences is a great way for students to share in their own words their goals, strategies, and progress. You can also offer guidance to make sure that they choose effective strategies and that their goals align with the curriculum.

As students become more comfortable with setting and achieving goals, gradually allow them to develop more independence. Ultimately, students should be able to set their own goals and select the achievement strategy that works for them.

You can use the following suggestions to scaffold goal-setting for students at different levels:

Beginning: Provide goals students should work toward based on curriculum criteria. Offer strategies for them to use to achieve goals.

Intermediate: Provide a "bank" of possible goals that align with curriculum criteria and allow students to choose which to work on. Work together with students to choose goal-achievement strategy.

Advanced: Provide students with open-ended prompts. Confer with students to make sure their goals align with the curriculum and that they have set a clear strategy for achieving their goals.

Setting Goals
Teach students to set goals that meet the **S.M.A.R.T.** requirements:

GOALS	DEFINITION	EXAMPLE
Specific	goals should be very focused.	• For example: *Improve vocabulary* is not a specific goal. • *Write down three unfamiliar words from a reading assignment and look them up in the dictionary* is much more specific.
Measurable	goals should be in small, concrete steps so that it's clear when the student is making progress.	• For example: *Understand what I read* is not a measurable goal. • *Identify the main idea in a text and write it in my own words* can be measured.
Achievable	goals must be manageable and progress-oriented.	• For example: *Always use correct spelling* is a daunting prospect. • *Practice correctly spelling words [the student] misspelled in an assignment* is much more manageable.
Relevant	goals should relate to the assignment and to the curriculum. Students will most likely need guidance from teachers to set goals that are relevant.	• Setting goals about skills unrelated to an assignment or setting goals that don't target areas in which the student needs improvement both fall outside the realm of relevant.
Time-bound	just like goals must be measurable, they must also have a set time frame so that students can track their progress.	• For example: *Read more* is not a specific or time-bound goal. *Read 50 pages*, is more specific but not time-bound. Students could take any amount of time to read those 50 pages. • Adding the clause *per week* and using other time constraints will help students to monitor their progress and adjust their strategies and goals as they need to. • *Read 50 pages per week* is a much more effective goal.

Student-Led Conferences

Student-led conferences are a great way to check how students perceive their own progress and to allow them to share their achievements, challenges, goals, and strategies. You can also offer guidance to make sure that they choose effective strategies and that their goals align with the curriculum. Here are some guiding questions you can ask to help them in the right direction:

- What are your strengths?
- What difficulties do you think you might encounter?
- How do you think you could work through those difficulties?
- Did you meet your goal?
- What did you do to meet your goal?

Make sure to let students think the questions and solutions through on their own before you make suggestions. Over time, students should begin to internalize strategies you suggest and be able to apply those strategies to accomplishing other goals in the future.

Written Self-Assessment

Teachers should offer frequent opportunities for students to self-assess in the classroom. Allowing students to use a few minutes before and after a class activity to pre-plan, strategize, and evaluate progress can help get students in the habit of constantly evaluating their development. This evaluation process can be done informally, by simply allowing students to brainstorm and write down their ideas before and after an assignment, or it can be more structured by using rubrics. Formal rubrics can help students of all levels to measure their progress for larger assignments, long-term goals, or large projects. Large projects should be broken down into distinct, individual steps, and students should evaluate themselves at each step.

Types of Self-Assessment Rubrics

Rubrics use many styles and formats to target students' specific needs. Here are a few examples of basic rubrics:

- A **skill/strategy-specific rubric** can help students focus on one or two specific skills over the course of one or more assignment(s).
- A **self-evaluation form** with open-response questions can be tailored to almost any kind of assignment with a focus on one or more skills.
- A **project-based rubric** can be used to focus on developing many skills in a reading workshop or large project.

Student/Team: _____   Date: _____

Social Action: Giving Big
Use this scoring guide to assess the student/team based on the final project.

STEPS	Needs Improvement 1	Average 2	Good 3	Excellent 4	Score/Comments
1. Brainstorm ideas	• Did not consider people, projects, causes, or local organizations when brainstorming a worthy cause.	• Considered people, projects, causes, or local organizations when brainstorming a worthy cause.	• Considered people, projects, causes, and local organizations when brainstorming a worthy cause.	• Used online resources to brainstorm a cause. • Considered people, projects, causes, and local organizations.	
2. Evaluate your options	• Chose one of the ideas from Step 3 but did not judge it against the contest criteria.	• Reviewed the ideas from Step 3. • Considered which idea the team is most excited about. • Wrote about the team's choice for a worthy cause.	• Reviewed the ideas from Step 3 and judged them based on the contest criteria. • Considered which idea the team is most excited about. • Wrote about the team's choice for a worthy cause.	• Reviewed the ideas from Step 3 and judged them based on the contest criteria. • Considered which idea the team is most excited about. • Wrote a complete sentence about the team's choice for a worthy cause.	
3. Make a plan and enter the contest	• Identified the cause but did not explain goals, information needed, or resources needed. • Did not identify all the steps to be taken to contribute to the cause. • Did not complete the entry form in the Resource Bank.	• Used the form to identify the cause, goals, information needed, and resources needed. • Identified a few steps to be taken to accomplish the goal. • Completed the entry form in the Resource Bank.	• Used the form to identify the cause, goals, information needed, and resources needed. • Identified the steps to be taken to accomplish the goal. • Reviewed the contest rules and completed the entry form, using the sample as a model. • Included specific details and examples in the entry form.	• Used the form to identify the cause, goals, information needed, and resources needed. • Identified the steps to accomplish the goal. • Reviewed the contest rules and completed the entry form, using the sample as a model. • Included specific details and examples in the entry form. • Prepared an organized presentation for the class.	
				Total	/20

READ180 Universal | Assessment

Use a project-based assessment rubric like this to focus on multiple strategies encountered during a performance task.

Consider these guidelines when developing self-assessment rubrics:

- Set concrete targets for students to measure themselves against.
- Focus on developing one skill over time or on the development of many skills within one assignment.
- Use rubrics as benchmarks for individual steps within a project.
- Detail clear criteria for each level of mastery within each skill being evaluated.
- Provide as much or as little guidance as students need.

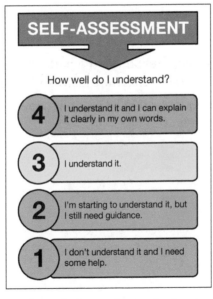

SELF-ASSESSMENT

How well do I understand?

4 I understand it and I can explain it clearly in my own words.

3 I understand it.

2 I'm starting to understand it, but I still need guidance.

1 I don't understand it and I need some help.

Sample rubric showing four levels of mastery.

Incorporating Test-Taking Practice Into Instruction

READ 180 students may have had uncomfortable test-taking experiences and lack the strategies and confidence needed to experience success on formal reading assessments. Help students build confidence and improve performance by explicitly teaching test-taking strategies and tailoring assessments to meet individual student needs.

Building Confidence With Instruction and Practice

READ 180 develops the following skills and strategies to build student success:

- Developing rapid word recognition to increase fluency and comprehension
- Reading and analyzing texts from various genres and with different structures
- Building vocabulary—especially high-utility words used in content-area texts
- Using comprehension and self-monitoring strategies with challenging text
- Developing skill and fluency in several writing types

Preparing Students for Assessments

Increase students' testing comfort level by incorporating test-taking strategies into instruction throughout the year. Begin by familiarizing students with testing procedures and terminology. For example, model how to read specific directions and question formats.

Assessment Strategies & Practice

Before each Interim and End-of-Workshop Assessment, teach the test-taking strategies lesson recommended in the Workshop Planning Guide. These lessons build students' familiarity with the most widely used types of tests and question/answer formats and will help students build confidence and ease with taking tests.

- Integrate test preparation when a particular skill is taught so that students make the connection between what they learn and how it will be tested.
- Model and frequently remind students how to read and interpret directions for tasks throughout the day.
- Review results from previous tests to customize your teaching strategies.

Inside an Assessment Strategies & Practice Lesson

Each Assessment Strategies & Practice lesson provides step-by-step instruction for tackling the types of items found on the Next Generation assessments. Many students will be unfamiliar with these question types and need this added instruction and practice. Go to **Resources** in HMH Teacher Central to access these lessons.

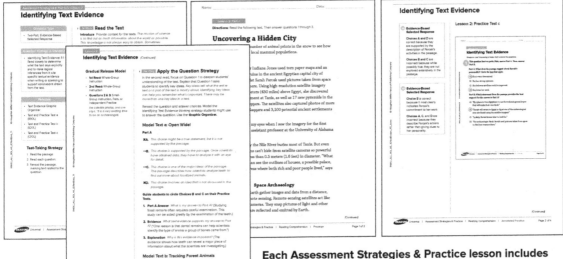

Each Assessment Strategies & Practice lesson includes instruction, an annotated graphic organizer, and an annotated practice test.

Open Wide!

What's in a tooth? Teeth contain mouthfuls of information about an animal.

by Natalie Smith

Teeth—they help us chew our food and speak clearly, and they give us our dazzling smiles. Some animals use their teeth for other functions, such as fighting enemies or cutting down plants to build homes. But for scientists, teeth have another benefit: they tell secrets. A peek inside an animal's mouth can tell researchers everything from what the animal eats to how old it is.

Tough Teeth

When scientists dig for fossils of ancient animals, they often look for dental remains. Teeth last much longer than other bones, which can break down over time.

"Bones are porous, or have many tiny holes, while teeth are solid," explains Robert Feranec, a fossil expert at the New York State Museum in Albany, New York. This means that as bones become fossils, they can wear away more quickly than teeth.

Teeth also have an added layer of protection: a hard, white covering called enamel. Enamel is what helps keep teeth from chipping when you bite down on a nut or a crunchy chip. The substance is so hard it can last for millions of years!

Dental Records

Why can finding an ancient tooth be so exciting for a scientist? One reason is that dental remains can help scientists identify the type of animal a group of bones came from. Each animal species has a unique set of teeth. They vary by number, size, shape, and organization. A

Tracking Forest Animals

One teen counts the number of animal prints in the snow to see how reforestation benefits local mammal populations.

by Sara Goudarzi

When 16-year-old Maia Persche needed an idea for a science project, she turned to her own backyard. Maia lives near Baraboo Hills in southern Wisconsin. Early settlers cut down much of the forest for farmland. But since the 1960s, the Nature Conservancy and local environmentalists have been working to restore the forest. This will protect songbirds, which rely on the habitat for nesting.

These reforestation projects seem to have helped bird populations. But what about other critters? Maia chose to study the forest's mammals to find out. "I was interested to see how mammals would respond to their habitat changing," she says.

Growing Stages

Maia researched locations for studying the animals before she began. She found a 1.4 square kilometer (337 acre) preserve called Pine Hollow. This piece of land would work well for her project because it contains three distinct types of forest.

Pine Hollow has two reforested areas of different ages. One area was replanted 15 years ago. The other was replanted 4 years ago. There's also an area of mature, undisturbed woodland. This area would serve as Maia's control. These three stages of tree growth would help Maia determine which kind of forest the mammals liked best. She suspected that the most mammals would be found in the mature forest. She thought she would find the fewest in the youngest 4-year-old plant

Uncovering a Hidden City

One teen counts the number of animal prints in the snow to see how reforestation benefits local mammal populations.

by Corey Binns

The movie character Indiana Jones used torn paper maps and an old diary to discover ruins in the ancient Egyptian capital city of Tanis. But archaeologist Sarah Parcak used pictures taken from space to find lost treasure there. Using high-resolution satellite imagery taken from 690 kilometers (430 miles) above Egypt, she discovered an unexcavated settlement at Tanis, as well as 17 new pyramids in the Egyptian region of Saqqara. The satellites also captured photos of more than 1,000 tombs in Saqqara and 3,100 potential ancient settlements across Egypt.

"I could not believe my eyes when I saw the imagery for the first time," says Parcak, an assistant professor at the University of Alabama at Birmingham.

Sediment carried by the Nile River buries most of Tanis. But even sediment-covered ruins can't hide from satellite cameras so powerful they can see objects less than 0.5 meters (1.6 feet) in diameter. "What is exciting is that we can see the outlines of houses, a possible palace, buildings, and even areas where both rich and poor people lived," says Parcak.

Space Archaeology

Satellites orbiting Earth gather images and data from a distance, a technique called remote sensing. Remote-sensing satellites act like sophisticated digital cameras. They snap pictures of light and other forms of energy that are reflected and emitted by Earth.

(Continued)

Differentiate Instruction: Each lesson includes grade-level passages at three different levels—Text a, Grades 3–5; Text b, Grades 6–8; Text c, Grades 9–12.

Tips for Administering Assessments

READ 180 offers a variety of assessment opportunities. In addition to daily assessment of students with the *READ 180* Student Application, students demonstrate learning through the HMH *Reading Inventory, Reading Counts!* quizzes, and *READ 180* Workshop Assessments.

HMH *Reading Inventory*

The Reading Inventory test provides a non-threatening environment for testing. The following features are built into *The Reading Inventory* test:

- Questions are not timed. Students are not pressured to answer questions as quickly as possible to complete the test. In addition, students can exit the test if they become fatigued and resume the test the next day.

- Students are permitted to skip up to three questions per test and are not penalized for skipping questions.

- Students can take a practice test to ensure that they understand the testing procedures.

- Most districts establish "testing windows" that extend for multiple days. Maximize on these testing windows by guiding students to select a day within the testing window that feels most comfortable for them to take the test.

Reading Counts! Quizzes

Reading Counts! quizzes are designed as short, motivational assessments of comprehension. Students can typically finish a quiz in one 20-minute rotation. You may wish to adjust the assessment environment to best meet the needs of your students:

- Allow students to retake quizzes. If a student has an unsuccessful attempt at a quiz, conference with the student to review quiz results and check comprehension, then allow the student to attempt the quiz again.

- Allow students to use completed reading logs, graphic organizers, or QuickWrites during their quiz.

- For students who experience multiple unsuccessful quiz attempts, consider printing out a copy of a *Reading Counts!* quiz and having the student complete the printed quiz while reading the book. Review responses and rationale with students prior to administering a quiz on the computer.

READ 180 Workshop Assessments

The *READ 180* Workshop Assessments are designed to be administered at the end of Part 1 and Part 2 of each *ReaL Book* Workshop. Like *The Reading Inventory, READ 180* Workshop Assessments are untimed so that students do not feel pressured to complete the test in one sitting.

- Consider administering Level a tests at the beginning of the year and moving to Level b tests, or consider assigning levels based on student reading level. (For more information about these tests, go to **Resources** in HMH Teacher Central and download the *READ 180 Workshop Assessments Introduction*.)

- Constructed-response items and writing prompts are optional. Consider which students may be hindered by being required to answer these types of questions.

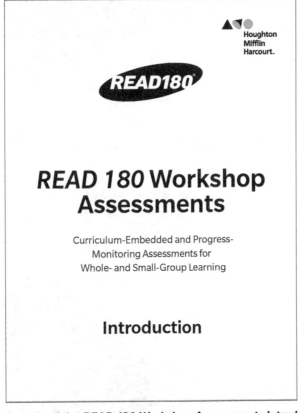

Download the *READ 180 Workshop Assessments Introduction* for additional assessment support strategies.

Data Analytics & Communication

Understand how to use actionable *READ 180* data analytics and reports to monitor skills mastery, measure growth, diagnose areas of difficulty, and individualize instruction. Learn about the various assessment tools and rubrics to grade students and share progress.

Meeting Teachers' Reporting Needs

As students participate in *READ 180,* data is collected about their use and performance in the program. Access this data through reports located in the Data Dashboard on HMH Teacher Central. These reports will enable you to monitor progress and plan daily instruction.

Data is collected and reported from the following components:

- *READ 180* Student Application
- *READ 180* Workshop Assessments
- HMH *Reading Inventory*
- *Reading Counts!* quizzes
- HMH *Phonics Inventory*

Putting Reports Data to Work

Reports are designed for flexible use. You can specify a time period for data you wish to view, sort, save, and print. Data can be used to diagnose student needs, track progress, determine instructional pacing, and differentiate instruction.

Sharing Data

Reports communicate data on classes or individual students, making it easy to share with others. Reports can also be used during conferences to help students set goals and develop accountability for their reading progress.

A parent report is available for *READ 180.* This report enable you to update parents and caregivers about their child's reading progress and involve them in their child's continued reading success. Reports can also help inform meaningful conversations with your school administrators about your classroom and students.

Purposeful Reporting

The following table describes specific purposes of some of the *READ 180* reports available through HMH Teacher Central.

Sample Reports	Purpose
• **Lexile Proficiency and Growth**	• Plan for differentiated instruction • Set and monitor reading goals • Match students to texts
• ***READ 180* Workshop Assessment**	• Identify class and/or student skill strengths and weaknesses • Group students by skill needs • Set and monitor instructional goals
• ***READ 180* Student Application** • **Independent Reading**	• Monitor student participation in programs • Track student progress and achievement • Set and monitor reading goals
• **Lexile Proficiency and Growth Parent**	• Introduce *READ 180* to families • Share progress updates • Facilitate discussions at parent-teacher conferences • Offer recommendations for family member involvement in student reading progress
• **Acceleration**	• Track to what extent implementation metrics are on target • Set and monitor reading goals
• **Academic Behavior and Mindset**	• monitor student behaviors through self-assessment, teacher observation, and data-driven behaviors

Managing Reports in the Data Dashboard

Select the Data Dashboard tab to access student analytics and real-time progress metrics to monitor student performance and adjust instruction.

Accessing Class or Student Reports

You have the option to view either Class or Student Reports from the Data Dashboard.

- When you first arrive at the Data Dashboard, the Class Reports screen will show the Lexile Proficiency and Growth Report as the default display.
- To view a student report, click a student from the pull-down menu under **Show Reports For.**

Viewing and Printing Report Data

The Data Dashboard includes features to support practical use of each report. Locate each of the following features in this report.

1. **Multiple Formats** View each report in both a graphic and tabular format to support easy interpretation and analysis.

2. **Summary** The report Summary presents high-level take-aways based on the report's specific data set.

3. **Sortable Data** Sort the data in each column for ease of use.

4. **Colored dots** Color-coded dots provide information about each student's performance: Advanced, Proficient, Basic, and Below Basic

5. **Celebration and Support Indicators** A green up-arrow next to a student's name indicates a point of success— the average Lexile measure increased. The message "No Growth" displays if the average Lexile measure decreased.

6. **Print Option** Click **Print Report** to export a printable PDF to submit as a hard copy or email as an attachment. Choose batch printing to print a report for all students.

Establishing a Reports Analysis Plan

READ 180 provides a comprehensive suite of reports for instructional planning, progress monitoring, and summative assessment. Establishing a data analysis plan fosters a seamless integration of using data and informing instruction. As part of your plan, consider creating a schedule with specific times to access and analyze reports.

Purposeful Reporting

Certain reports are helpful at different points within the school year. Consider when it is most appropriate to analyze reports for monitoring student progress or making instructional decisions. Decide which reports are useful to share with students, families, and administrators.

As you analyze reports, keep track of what you learned and what actions you took in a data notebook. In this way you can refer back to previous data-driven plans to more easily track student performance and progress.

Establishing a Data Analysis Schedule

Use your school calendar, your *ReaL Book* Workshop Planning Guides, and your testing calendar to establish a schedule for accessing and analyzing reports.

Create a data analysis schedule:

1. Include the Lexile Proficiency and Growth reports first; plan to access them before and after each *Reading Inventory* testing window.

2. Include reports used for grading next. Plan to access these reports near the end of each grading period.

3. Consider the pacing of your Workshops. Plan to make grouping decisions based on reports before each Checkpoint. Access *READ 180* Workshop Assessment reports at the Interim and End-of-Workshop Checkpoints.

4. Establish days to conference with students. Access reports for student conferencing prior to those conference days.

Establishing a Reports Analysis Plan (continued)

READ 180 Reporting Overview

Each day students log on to the *READ 180* Student App, data of their program use and progress in key skill areas is captured. This information can be accessed for individual students, or a class.

READ 180 reports are flexible, allowing you to view and sort specific information to monitor progress and target instruction to meet the specific needs of students, especially during Small-Group Learning.

The following sections summarize the types of information that can be found in *READ 180* reports.

1. Completion and Participation Data

Multiple data points provide an update of student activity in the various components of *READ 180*. Metrics such as Segments completed, Average session (min.), and Lexile measure growth can be reviewed and correlated.

Student completion pattern analysis is especially important for those not showing positive Lexile growth. Reviewing data points such as average daily use of the Student Application, segment completion, and books completed from *Reading Counts!* quizzes can help ensure that students are participating appropriately in *READ 180*.

Conferences with students that are often absent or not meeting minimum participation benchmarks may be necessary. These students may need help setting and tracking goals for attendance and daily participation.

2. Performance and Progress Monitoring Data

READ 180 reports also allow you to track student progress in key areas that affect reading ability. (See these key areas in the chart on the next page.) These reports will help you monitor students' improvement in both foundational reading skills and higher-order thinking skills to inform grouping and differentiation decisions. Use Small-Group Learning to target specific strategies and skills for a few students. If you find that a large number of students need support with a particular strategy, plan a Whole-Group lesson.

Strand	Small-Group Rotation
Reading Comprehension	• Focuses on a wide range of comprehension strategies practiced in the Student App, the *ReaL Book*, and Independent Reading texts including identifying central idea and details, making inferences, and analyzing text structures.
Language	• Focuses on language skills and strategies covered in various components of *READ 180* such as vocabulary knowledge, use of context clues, and syntax and grammar.
Fluency	• Focuses on students' ability to fluently read connected text in passages by measuring student prosody and accuracy through the calculation of a Words Correct Per Minute (WCPM) score.
Word Recognition	• Focuses on students' ability to accurately and quickly decode words. Reports generate common error types as well as example words that provide evidence of these deficiencies.
Spelling	• Focuses on students' ability to accurately spell words, along with common error types with examples for each.
Writing	• Focuses on student writing performance and progress based on rubric-driven teacher evaluation of assignments in the Student Application and assessments such as the *READ 180* End-of-Workshop Assessment.

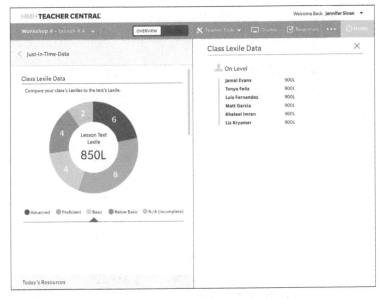

Access Just-in-Time Data in the Digital Teacher's Edition.

Just-In-Time Data

In addition to reports, include Just-in-Time Data in your analysis. These snapshots show real-time, at-a-glance data. For example, use the Class Lexile Data to quickly compare a student's Lexile measure with the Lexile measure of the text they are reading that day to determine readiness.

READ 180 Data Stories

The following case studies represent four possible paths through a single year in *READ 180*. Throughout this section of the *Assessment & Analytics Guide,* we will expand upon and interpret certain reports through the lens of one or two of these students.

DATA STORY

The Excelling Student

Student: Angelika Chavez
Grade: 7
Initial Lexile: 950
Final Lexile: 1050
Final Performance Standard: Proficient

Angelika began the year with a Lexile measure in the Basic range. To stretch her comprehension skills, Angelika's teacher encouraged her to read books during Independent Reading that were on level or challenging for her current Lexile measure. Angelika participated fully in *READ 180*; she rarely missed a class and was vocal during Small-Group Learning. While she still had some difficulty with reading comprehension, by the end of the year Angelika moved to the Proficient performance level and is eligible to exit *READ 180*.

[See an example of one of Angelika's reports on Page 160.]

Possible indicators of an Excelling student:

- Solid growth in Lexile measure across the year
- Leveling up in the *READ 180* Student App
- High performance on Workshop Assessments
- High quiz success rate for *Reading Counts!* quizzes
- Frequent "on track" assessments by teacher in Observer tool

DATA STORY

The Progressing Student

Student: Armen Serrato
Grade: 7
Initial Lexile: 695
Final Lexile: 775
Final Performance Standard: Basic

Armen began the year with a Lexile measure in the Below Basic range. His teacher helped him set a goal to move up one performance level by the end of the year. English is his second language, and he struggles in particular with vocabulary and spelling. By tracking his growth and providing additional support during Small-Group Learning, Armen moved to the Basic performance level by the end of the year.

[See an example of one of Armen's reports on Page 167.]

Possible indicators of a Progressing student:

- Moderate growth in Lexile across the year
- Leveling up in *READ 180* Student App after midyear
- Improved performance on Workshop Assessments across the year
- Good quiz success rate for *Reading Counts!* quizzes
- Occasional "nearly there" assessments by teacher in Observer tool
- May show some inconsistency across skills and performance

The Static Student

Student: Taunya Williams
Grade: 7
Initial Lexile: 800
Final Lexile: 810
Final Performance Standard: Basic

Taunya began the year with a Lexile measure in the Basic range and ended the year with a Lexile measure in the Basic range. While she does fairly well in the *READ 180* Student App, she has remained in the same Level all year. Taunya moves very slowly through the Student App, and she often requires multiple attempts to pass a *Reading Counts!* quiz. She struggles with reading comprehension and writing. Taunya's teacher may have been able to help Taunya more by providing her with additional support during Independent Reading.

[See an example of one of Taunya's reports on pages **161**.]

Possible indicators of a Static student:

- Minimal change in Lexile measure across the year
- May not level up in *READ 180* Student App
- No change or drop in scores on Workshop Assessments across the year
- Poor quiz success rate for *Reading Counts!* quizzes
- Frequent "not yet" or "nearly there" assessments by teacher in Observer tool

The Struggling Student

Student: Shawn Metz
Grade: 7
Initial Lexile: 620
Final Lexile: 560
Final Performance Standard: Below Basic

Shawn began the year with a Lexile in the Below Basic range and ended the year with a Lexile in the Below Basic range. He has completed very few *READ 180* Student App segments. He has never passed a *Reading Counts!* quiz on the first try. He struggles with many aspects of reading and appears very frustrated. Shawn's teacher may be able to help him by administering *The Phonics Inventory*; it is possible that Shawn is better suited for *System 44*.

[See an example of one of Shawn's reports on page **166**.]

Possible indicators of a struggling student:

- Low performance across all components of *READ 180*
- No growth in Lexile measure across the year
- Extremely slow movement through *READ 180* Student App
- No change or drop in scores on Workshop Assessments across the year
- Poor quiz success rate for *Reading Counts!* quizzes
- Frequent "not yet" assessments by teacher in Observer tool

Data Analytics & Communication

Lexile Proficiency and Growth Report *(Class)*

Purpose

This report displays the average class Lexile measure at two points, as well as the average class Lexile growth. It also shows the expected growth range for each student based on initial Lexile measure.

	First Test				Last Test			Growth	
Student	Grade	Lexile®	Level	Date	Lexile®	Level	Date	Expected	Actual
Bracco, Christine	7	800L	Basic	9/3/16	860L	Basic	6/21/17	35–65L	60L
Chavez, Angelika	7	950L	Basic	9/2/16	1050L	Proficient	6/21/17	30–60L	100L
Williams, Taunya	7	800L	Basic	9/3/16	810L	Basic	6/21/17	35–65L	10L
Average		807L			873L				73L

Understand the Data

1 **Time Period**
Customize time periods to review results across the entire school year or any other meaningful time span.

2 **Average Lexile Growth**
Average Lexile increase from the first test to the last test within selected time period for the entire class. Average declines in Lexile display "No Growth".

3 **Students Who Improve/No Growth**
These two summary statistics report (a) the number of students in the class who have improved their Lexile score from first test to last test, and (b) the number of students who have not shown growth.

4 **Performance Level Breakdown**
The performance level breakdown graphs the percentage of students in each performance level band on the first and last test within the selected time period.

Each horizontal bar is a performance level band, and the length represents the number and percent of students in the class who fell into this performance level for the given test.

5 **Performance Level**
Student's reading level based on the four *Reading Inventory* performance standards: Advanced, Proficient, Basic, and Below Basic. Performance standard Lexile ranges vary by grade level.

6 **First Test**
Lexile score, performance **Level**, and **Date** of first *Reading Inventory* test within selected time period.

7 **Last Test**
Lexile score, performance **Level**, and **Date** of last *Reading Inventory* test within selected time period. N/A indicates a second test was not completed within selected time period.

8 **Expected Lexile Growth**
Range of expected Lexile growth between the first and last administration under typical conditions based on grade level and reading achievement.

9 **Actual Lexile Growth**
Lexile increase from the first test to the last test within selected time period with an indicator of whether students met or exceeded their growth goals. Declines in Lexile between two tests are indicated in parentheses.

Use the Data

WHO: Teachers

WHEN: Report data is updated in real time. Review after each *Reading Inventory* administration and monitor as necessary.

HOW: You can use the information from this report to:

Monitor Growth

- Monitor how much students need to grow to achieve grade-level proficiency.
- Discuss growth rates and help students set appropriate yearly Lexile measure growth goals.* See Establishing *Reading Inventory* Growth Targets for more information.

Target Support

- Target additional support to students who are not showing strong gains or whose current *Reading Inventory* scores are below grade-level expectations.
- Carefully analyze results for students whose scores have declined.

Note that Lexile growth is typically greater for younger and/or less proficient readers but may be influenced by many factors, including language proficiency, developmental ability, and degree of instructional intervention, among others.

Lexile Proficiency and Growth Report *(Student)*

Purpose

This report displays student's Lexile measure growth based on *Reading Inventory* results over a selected time period.

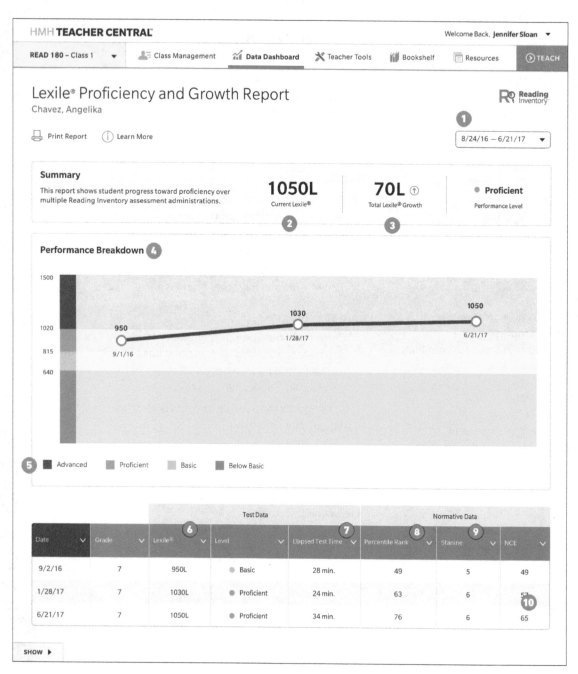

Understand the Data

1 Time Period

Customize time periods to review results across the entire school year or any other meaningful time span.

2 Current Lexile

Lexile score from most recent *Reading Inventory* test within selected time period.

3 Total Lexile Growth

Lexile increase from the first test to the last test within selected time period. Declines in Lexile are indicated with "No Growth."

4 Performance Breakdown

The performance breakdown graph plots Lexile across *Reading Inventory* tests. The horizontal axis represents time and the vertical axis represents Lexile, divided into performance level bands. Each dot indicates the Lexile score and date for that test.

5 Performance Level

Student's reading level based on the four *Reading Inventory* performance standards: Advanced, Proficient, Basic, and Below Basic. Performance standard Lexile ranges vary by grade level.

6 Lexile

Lexile score for given *Reading Inventory* test.

7 Elapsed Test Time

Test duration for *Reading Inventory* test. Test times under 15 minutes are considered unusually low and indicated with an icon.

8 Percentile Rank

Percentage of students from a national sample who received lower scores than this student on this test on a scale of 1 to 99. For example, a student who scores at the 65th percentile performed as well or better than 65 percent of the norm group.

9 Stanine

A standardized score that indicates a student's relative standing in a norm group. Stanines 1, 2, and 3 are below average; stanines 4, 5, and 6 are average; and stanines 7, 8, and 9 are above average.

10 NCE (Normal Curve Equivalent)

A comparison of student's rate of progress to the norm, based on a national sample. Students making exactly one year of progress in one year of instruction earn a score of 0. Those progressing faster earn a score from 1 to 99, depending on the rate of increase.

Use the Data

WHO: Teachers

WHEN: Report data is updated in real time. Review after each *Reading Inventory* administration, and monitor as necessary.

HOW: Use the information from this report to review comprehensive student performance on *Reading Inventory* and monitor progress trends.

Monitor Growth

- Analyze growth across multiple *Reading Inventory* tests.
- Compare performance standards with grade-level performance.
- Discuss growth rates and help students set *Reading Inventory* growth goals. See Establishing *Reading Inventory* Growth Targets for more information.
- Use online certificates to recognize growth.

Target Support

- Prepare students for the *Reading Inventory* test by discussing previous test results.
- Explain to students that subsequent tests begin at their current Lexile level, so initial questions may seem more or less challenging.

READ 180 Student Application Report *(Student)*

Purpose

This report displays student status, usage, and performance in the *READ 180* Student Application.

Understand the Data

1 Time Period
Customize time periods to review results across the entire school year or any other meaningful time span.

2 Current Level
Current level in *READ 180* Student App.

3 Average Session Length
Average time (in minutes) that student spends in the *READ 180* Student App per session (day).

4 Sessions Completed
Total number of sessions completed within the designated time period.

5 Zone Activity Performance
Graph displays performance in each zone activity within the *READ 180* Student App.

The light blue bar represents the average score for this zone across all completed segments in this time period. The dark blue bar represents the student's scores on the current segment. N/A indicates that this zone is not yet completed. Length of bar corresponds with score on activity.

6 Progress Table
This table chronologically lists each segment completed or in progress for this time period.

The **Implementation** columns include: **Segment, Level, Date Started, Date Completed,** and the total **Sessions** (days) it took for the student to complete this segment.

The **Performance** columns include performance in each activity zone (% correct).

Bottom row includes averages (% correct) across all segments.

Use the Data

WHO: Teachers, Students, and Caregivers

WHEN: Monthly

HOW: You can use the information from this report in the following ways:

Monitor Participation and Progress
- Track progress throughout the year, noting improvement in scores and rate of completion.
- Review performance results to determine areas of challenge, and provide additional support as needed.
- Conference with students to determine cause for low scores or a high number of sessions per segment.

Analyze Results

Data Story: The Excelling Student
Student: Angelika Chavez

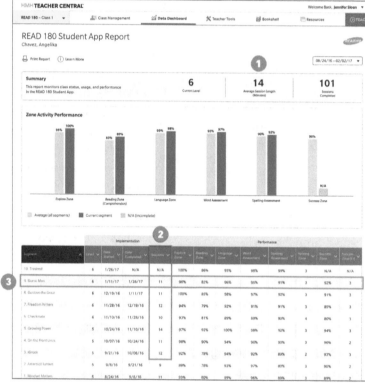

Angelika has completed **10** segments and her scores have improved over time. She occasionally struggles in the Reading zone. Identify causes and ways to provide additional reading comprehension support.

	Data Point	Data Analysis	Next Steps
1	Angelika's zone activity performance bar graph shows overall high performance, with even higher performance on her current segment.	Angelika's high scores and current performance indicate that she is doing very well in the Student App. You may want to consider her a candidate for a manual level promotion.	Before adjusting Student App levels, ensure that she is earning high scores in all zones. Celebrate success. Encourage Angelika to challenge herself with related Independent Reading books or eReads.
2	Angelika's scores in the Reading Zone are lower than other zones. However, her scores show improvement over time.	Angelika's lower Reading Zone score may suggest particular difficulty with comprehension. However, her improvement over time is positive and promising for continued improvement.	Due to her lower comprehension scores, reconsider the manual promotion and allow her to remain in Level 5. Celebrate improvement in reading comprehension. Provide additional support as needed, and during conferences ask Angelika to articulate the types of challenges she is facing.
3	Angelika leveled up prior to her 6th segment. Her scores dropped on this segment.	Angelika leveled up in the Student App due to high performance. It is normal for scores to drop a little once a student is in a higher level due to increased text complexity.	Celebrate the level promotion change with Angelika. Monitor her performance to ensure that she is comfortable at this level.

Analyze Results

Data Story: The Static Student
Student: Taunya Williams

Taunya has completed **seven** segments. She progresses slowly and struggles in the Reading and Writing zones. Monitor her to make sure she stays on-task during the Student App rotation.

	Data Point	Data Analysis	Next Steps
1	Taunya has a low average session time (12).	If most of the class is maintaining appropriate session length, Taunya is likely off-task during this rotation.	Ask Taunya to track her daily progress. Monitor her during the Student App rotation to ensure that she is focusing on the task at hand.
2	Taunya has a high average number of sessions per segment (17).	Students should average 4-15 sessions per segment. Taunya is not progressing through segments as quickly as she should.	Conference with her to determine why she is spending so many sessions on each segment. Review additional reports to identify zones that she may have difficulty completing.
3	Taunya performed unusually low in her 6th segment.	Taunya may have had extenuating circumstances that affected her ability to perform this month. Students may show a drop in scores after vacations such as winter break.	Conference with Taunya to determine why she demonstrated unusually low performance. Review Student App tips and procedures with the class each grading period, especially after long breaks.

READ 180 Workshop Assessment Report (Class)

Purpose

This report shows class results on one READ 180 Workshop Assessment. Results are displayed by level, strands, and strategies, and include teacher-scored items.

HMH **TEACHER CENTRAL**

Welcome Back, **Jennifer Sloan** ▼

| READ 180 – Class 1 ▼ | ▲ Class Management | 📊 Data Dashboard | 🔧 Teacher Tools | 📖 Bookshelf | 🗐 Resources | ▶ TEACH |

Workshop Assessment Report
Class 1

🖶 Print Report   ⓘ Learn More

① Workshop Assessment 4 ▼

Summary

This report summarizes student performance on strands and skills tested in a single Workshop Assessment.

② **78%** Average Test Score (Level A)

③ **74%** Average Test Score (Level B)

Cite Textual Evidence
Target Strategy

④ Assessment Averages   Reading   Language   Writing

Strand	Level A	Level B
Analyze People, Events, and Ideas	80%	75%
Author Point of View	77%	72%
Cite Textual Evidence	74%	75%
Metaphor	81%	76%
Text Structure	83%	81%
Integrating Texts	77%	72%

Level A (below grade level): 9 students   Level B (at grade level): 5 students

⑤ Strategy Results   Level A   Level B

| | | Reading | | | | | | Language | | | | |
Student Name ⌄	Test Date ⌄	Analyze People, Events, and Ideas ⌄	Author Point of View ⌄	Cite Textual Evidence ⌄	Metaphor ⌄	Text Structure ⌄	Integrate Texts ⌄	Denotation and Connotation ⌄	Word Choice ⌄	Verb Tense ⌄	Suffixes ⌄	Test Score ⌄
Bracco, Christine	1/20/17	● 5/5	● 3/3	2/3	3/4	2/2	● 3/3	1/2	1/1	5/6	1/1	87%
Felix, Tonya	1/20/17	4/5	● 3/3	● 3/3	3/4	2/2	● 3/3	2/2	1/1	4/6	1/1	87%
Fernandez, Luis	1/20/17	2/5	2/3	2/3	2/4	1/2	2/3	1/2	1/1	3/6	0/1	53%
Imran, Khaleel	1/20/17	● 5/5	2/3	● 3/3	3/4	2/2	● 3/3	2/2	1/1	5/6	1/1	90%
Krynski, Theo	1/20/17	4/5	● 3/3	2/3	● 4/4	2/2	● 3/3	2/2	1/1	4/6	1/1	77%
Metz, Shawn	1/20/17	3/5	1/3	● 0/3	2/4	0/2	1/3	2/2	1/1	3/6	0/1	87%
Ramirez, Gabrielle	1/20/17	● 5/5	2/3	● 3/3	● 4/4	2/2	2/3	1/2	1/1	● 6/6	1/1	90%
Sanchez, Rachel	1/20/17	4/5	● 3/3	● 3/3	● 4/4	2/2	2/3	2/2	1/1	5/6	0/1	43%
Williams, Taunya	1/20/17	4/5	2/3	2/3	● 4/4	2/2	2/3	2/2	0/1	5/6	0/1	90%
Level A Average		80%	77%	74%	81%	83%	77%	75%	93%	74%	67%	78%

⑥ Teacher Scored Items   Level A   Level B

Understand the Data

1 **Workshop Assessments**

Select which Workshop Assessment report data you want to view.

2 **Average Test Score (Level a and Level b)**

Average score for all students taking the Workshop Assessment, displayed by test Level a or b.

3 **Target Strategy**

Target strategy for class based on class-wide performance on the Workshop Assessment. Strategy with lowest average score will be designated as the target.

4 **Assessment Averages**

Select strand (Reading, Language, Writing) at the top of the graph.

Graph displays average scores on Workshop Assessment Strategies by Level. Each horizontal bar is a Workshop Assessment Level (a or b), and the length represents the average score on a given Strategy in the selected Strand.

5 **Strategy Results**

Select Level (a or b) at the top of the table.

Table displays **Test Date** and Workshop Assessment scores for multiple-choice items as a ratio of correct/total items by Strategy. Right-most column lists overall score (% correct). Bottom row includes overall averages (% correct) for selected Level by Strategy.

Green dots indicate high performance on a given strategy; red dots indicate low performance.

6 **Teacher-Scored Items**

Select Level (A or B) at the top of the table.

Table displays End-of-Workshop Assessment results for teacher-scored **Constructed-Response** items and **Extended Writing** (Writing Prompt). Scores are displayed as a ratio of points correct/total points by item type. Bottom row includes averages for selected Level.

Use the Data

WHO: Teachers (Class Report)

WHEN: After each Interim and End-of-Workshop Assessment

HOW: You can use the information from this report in the following ways:

Target Instruction

- If the majority of students struggled with a particular strategy, select an appropriate RDI lesson to deliver to the entire class during Whole-Group Learning at the End-of-Workshop Checkpoint.
- Use this report to inform grouping decisions.
- If a student is scoring well on the below-grade-level tests (Level a), consider assigning a Level b test the next time the student takes a Workshop Assessment.

Review Results

- Monitor test performance, and review individual student results as needed.

READ 180 Independent Reading Report *(Student)*

Purpose

This report provides an overview of a student's *Reading Counts!* quiz participation and progress.

Understand the Data

1 Time Period

Customize time periods to review results across the entire school year or any other meaningful time span.

2 Total Books Read

Total books read across all paperbacks, ebooks, audiobooks, and eReads where student passed the *Reading Counts!* quiz.

3 Total Words Read

Total words read across all Paperbacks, eBooks, Audiobooks, and eReads where student passed the *Reading Counts!* quiz.

4 Current Student Lexile

Student's most recent *Reading Inventory* score.

5 Words Read per Month

Graph displays the total number of words read per month. Bars represent each month and length indicates the number of words. Gray bars indicate a month that is currently in progress.

6 Quiz Table

Table chronologically lists all *Reading Counts!* quizzes for selected time period. Each book or eRead quiz can be attempted up to three times.

7 Book Information

Within the quiz table, these columns provide basic information about the reading materials corresponding to each *Reading Counts!* quiz. **Book Lexile** is the Lexile measure of each book or eRead. **Format** lists the type of book. Students can choose between paperbacks, eBooks, audiobooks, and eReads. **Type** is either **Literary** (fiction) or **Informational** (nonfiction). **Genre** identifies the genre of each text.

8 Student Rating

This smiley-face column indicates student rating of each book, ranging from 😐 to 😃.

9 Quiz Information

These columns provide information about the Quiz. **Quiz Type** can be **Standard** or **Challenge**. **Score** lists the % correct on the quiz. 70% is the default passing score. **Words Read** lists the number of words read for each book. **Quiz Points** indicates the number of points earned for this book. Each book and eRead is assigned a set point value. Students earn points for each quiz passed.

NOTE: Students must pass a quiz to earn Words Read *and* Points.

10 Averages (Totals)

The bottom row includes the averages and/or totals across all quizzes.

Use the Data

WHO: Teachers (Class Report)

WHEN: Once or twice a month

HOW: You can use the information from this report in the following ways:

Establish and Track Goals

- Conference with students regarding their progress. Celebrate success and encourage continued reading growth.
- Establish goals for words read, pages read, or books read for each student. Have students use this report to track progress toward that goal.

Share Results

- Add this report to student portfolios as a record of independent reading achievement.
- Print this report to share at conferences with parents or caregivers to provide more detail on students' progress.

Analyze Results

Data Story: The Struggling Student
Student: Shawn Metz

Shawn has not passed many *Reading Counts!* quizzes. Ensure he is reading books within his Lexile range, and set individual quiz goals based on his ability.

	Data Point	Data Analysis	Next Steps
❶	Shawn has only read three Independent Reading books.	Shawn is struggling with *Reading Counts!* quizzes. He may be reading too slowly to fully comprehend the text. He may also not be trying hard enough to pass quizzes.	Try to determine the cause for the low number of books read and investigate specific quiz results. Ask Shawn if he is really giving his best effort to pass a quiz.
❷	Shawn has attempted and failed a quiz on a book three times.	His second quiz was only one day after his first attempt.	If a student has an unsuccessful quiz attempt, provide additional support prior to allowing the student to take a quiz again.
❸	Shawn's average quiz score is 58%.	Shawn has attempted nine quizzes, but he has only passed three of them.	Try to bolster Shawn's confidence by having him take a print version of the test as practice, and do not count the score. Review results with him before he retakes the test on the computer.

Analyze Results

Data Story: The Progressing Student
Student: Armen Serrato

Armen has read five books. Encourage him to choose books that are just above his current Lexile measure to further develop his reading comprehension skills.

	Data Point	Data Analysis	Next Steps
1	Armen has read a total of 119,000 words in this time period.	Armen is reading extensively in the Independent Reading rotation.	Celebrate success and encourage continued reading growth.
2	Armen's average book Lexile score is 680L and his current Lexile score is 750L.	Armen is reading books on the lower end of his independent reading range.	Since Armen has been passing most of his quizzes, encourage him to select books that are slightly above his current Lexile.
3	Armen has passed five quizzes, but he has only chosen to take one Challenge quiz.	Armen could gain confidence by taking more Challenge quizzes.	Encourage Armen to "ramp it up" by taking more Challenge quizzes. Remind him that he is always able to retake a quiz if he does not pass it on the first attempt.

Data Analytics & Communication

READ 180 Observer Report

Purpose

This report summarizes student formative assessment scores in the Observer tool.

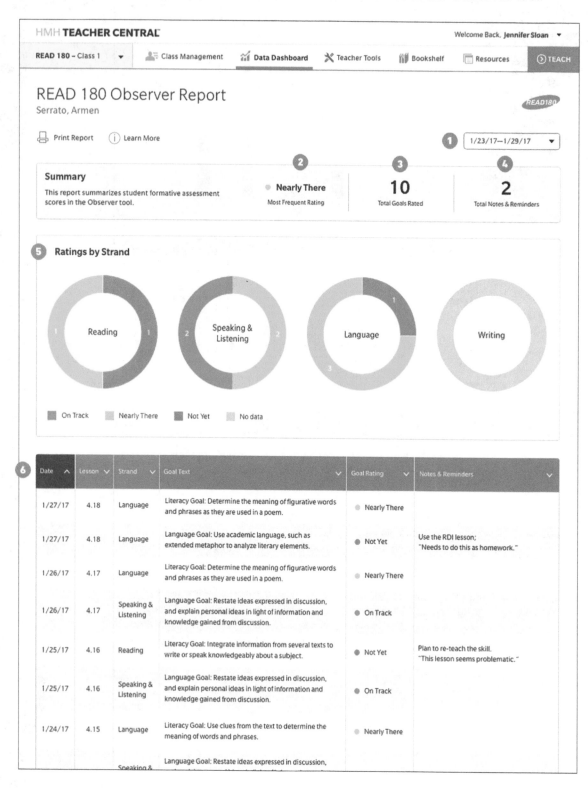

Understand the Data

1 **Time Period**

Customize time periods to review results across the entire school year or any other meaningful time span.

2 **Most Frequent Rating**

Displays the most common "goal rating" the student has received across rated goals. Students can receive a goal rating of **On Track**, **Nearly There**, or **Not Yet** for each goal.

3 **Total Goals Rated**

Total number of goals the teacher has rated in the Observer tool.

4 **Total Notes & Reminders**

Total number of notes and reminders entered into the Observer tool.

5 **Ratings by Strand**

Graph displays the number and proportion of each type of goal rating broken out by strand (Reading, Speaking & Listening, Language, or Writing).

6 **Observer Table**

Table chronologically lists all rated goals. Columns include **Date** of rating, **Lesson** number, **Strand**, **Goal Text** specifying the goal, **Goal Rating** (On Track, Nearly There, or Not Yet), and any **Notes & Reminders** the teacher has chosen to include.

Use the Data

WHO: Teachers

WHEN: Once or twice a month

HOW: You can use the information from this report in the following ways:

Monitor Student Progress

- Determine which strands and goals students are struggling with, and target instruction by providing additional support accordingly.
- When using the Digital Teacher's Edition, be sure to incorporate the Adopt Instruction strategies that are a part of each daily formative assessment.

Share Results

- Add this report to student portfolios as a record of overall student progress across strands.
- Print this report to share at conferences with parents or caregivers to provide more detail on students' progress.

Grading in *READ 180*

When grading, consider a student's complete progress and performance in the *READ 180* classroom. Balance grades from each of the rotations—Whole-Group, Small-Group, Independent Reading, and Student Application.

The Blended Learning Model

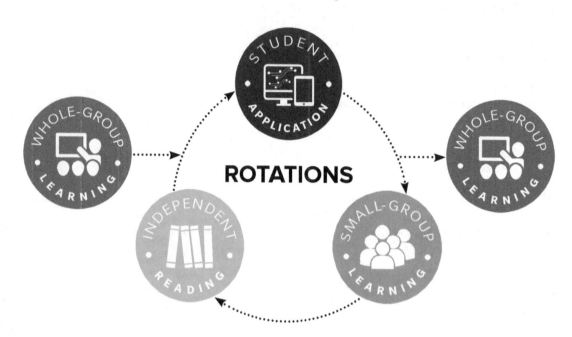

Setting Up a Grading System

When setting up your grade book for the year, consider how to balance grades and assignments from each of the rotations. When determining what data to use for grading, consider including Data Dashboard report results, Assignment Board results, as well as classroom artifacts not included on HMH Teacher Central. For example, in some READ 180 implementations students spend an equal amount of time in each rotation, so you may wish to balance the assignment weights as follows:

- **Whole-Group Learning:** 25%
- **Small-Group Learning:** 25%
- **Independent Reading:** 25%
- **Student Application:** 25%

If you choose to assign homework, such as an eReads article and accompanying QuickWrites, you may wish to add that assignment type and adjust weighting accordingly.

Grading Options

Review the following list of grading options when establishing your grade book for the school year. You may wish to include some or all of these assignment types when compiling grades for each student.

	Options	Data	Classroom Artifacts
SMALL-GROUP LEARNING / WHOLE-GROUP LEARNING	**WHOLE- AND SMALL-GROUP LEARNING**	• Formative Assessment results (Observer Report) • *READ 180* Interim Workshop assessment results • *READ 180* End-of-Workshop Assessment results	• *ReaL Book* Workshop Rubric • *ReaL Book* Writing Rubric • *ReaL Book* Career Project • Interim and End-of-Year Performance Tasks • Resources for Differentiated Instruction (RDI) lessons • Participation in daily lessons • Do Now/Wrap-Up activities
STUDENT APPLICATION	**STUDENT APPLICATION**	Analytics for: • Reading comprehension average • Implementation metrics • Performance metrics • Segments completed	• Writing Zone or Writing Prompt essays • Fluency Check recordings • Student Application Log • Daily focus/participation
INDEPENDENT READING	**INDEPENDENT READING**	Analytics for: • Reading progress • Quiz success	• Daily reading logs • QuickWrites • Graphic Organizers • Daily focus/participation • Projects or presentations

READ 180 Grading Form

To assign periodic grades, download the *READ 180* Grading Form from the Resources on HMH Teacher Central. Use *Reading Inventory* and *READ 180* reports, *ReaL Book*, and any other assignments to complete the form for each student. Store copies of completed forms in your data notebook to share with parents during conferences.

Completing the Grading Form

Follow these steps to complete the *READ 180* Grading Form for each of your students:

1. Decide which criteria on the Grading Form you want to factor into student grades. Use the blank rows to add any additional criteria. Cross out rows for any criteria that you do not want to consider.

2. Use *READ 180* reports, especially the Workshop Assessment Report, to identify a student's performance on each criterion that you are considering. Record the performance score as a percentage in the Grade column. Example: 85%.

3. Assign each criterion a weight in order to prioritize bigger assignments. Ask yourself: *Which of these criteria do I consider most important? Least important?* For accurate class assessment, apply the same weight to each criterion for every student. Record this percentage in the Weight column. Example: 25%.

4. Multiply each grade by the weight of importance. Convert percentages to decimals when multiplying. Example: 85% = .85. Record the results in the Subtotal column.

5. Add all subtotals together and multiply by 100. Record the result in the space for Final Grade. Convert this number to a letter grade if required.

READ 180 Grading Form

Complete the table below to determine a *READ 180* class grade for each of your students.

Criterion	Grade	Weight	Subtotal
Whole- and Small-Group Learning			
READ 180 Workshop Assessments Overall Score			
ReaL Book Workshop Rubric			
ReaL Book Writing Rubric			
Interim or End-of-Workshop Performance Task			
Daily Participation & Motivation (Observer Tool)			
Student Application			
Comprehension Tasks			
Language Score			
Context Task			
Fluency Check (Assignment Board)			
Writing Zone Score (Assignment Board)			
QuickWrites			
Daily Participation & Motivation (Teacher Observation)			
Independent Reading			
Reading Counts! Quiz Average			
QuickWrites & Graphic Organizers			
Daily Reading Log			
Daily Participation & Motivation (Teacher Observation)			
			_____ (100) = _____
Total			

FINAL GRADE: _____ %

FINAL LETTER GRADE: _____ %

READ180 Universal I Classroom Management I Grading Form I **Teacher Resource**

Use this Grading Form to help you determine final grades for a marking period.

Sharing Results With Students

When to Conference

Sharing progress data with students fosters student ownership and increases motivation. Schedule regular conferences with students. Use *READ 180*'s assessments results and student reports to update students on their progress, set goals, and celebrate achievement.

In a *READ 180* classroom, the best opportunity for student conferencing is during rotations on pre-determined days.

Near the end of each marking period.
Go to HMH Teacher Central to download a lesson or project associated with your current *ReaL Book* Workshop. Pull students one at a time from Small-Group Learning while the other students are working on the project.

When the daily schedule is shortened.
On days when the bell schedule is revised to allow for assemblies or meetings, your class may not have time to complete all rotations. If the class time is reduced enough to eliminate a rotation, consider moving students directly into rotations. Have students in the Small-Group Learning complete an independent activity while you conference one-on-one with students.

Determine which option best fits your classroom environment and communicate your conferencing plans to students. Establishing regular time within your schedule to conference with students creates a sense of stability and structure for students.

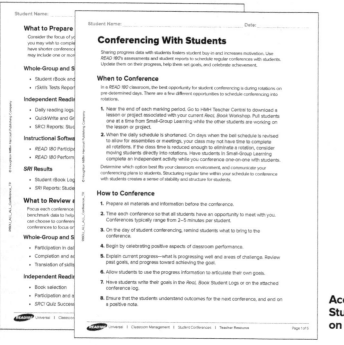

Access this Conferencing With Students packet in Resources on HMH Teacher Central.

How to Conference With Students

Consider the following suggestions as you plan student conferences.

1. Prepare all materials and information before the conference.

2. Time each conference so that all students have an opportunity to meet with you. Conferences typically range from 2–5 minutes per student.

3. On the day of student conferencing, remind students what to bring to the conference.

4. Begin by celebrating positive aspects of classroom performance.

5. Explain current progress—what is progressing well and areas of challenge. Review past goals and progress toward achieving the goal.

6. Allow students to use the progress information to articulate their own goals.

7. Have students write their goals in the *ReaL Book* Student Logs or on conference logs.

8. Ensure that the student understands outcomes for the next conference, and end on a positive note.

What to Prepare for a Student Conference

Consider the focus of your conference as you gather relevant information. During some conferences you may wish to complete a review of progress in each rotation, while at other times you may wish to have shorter conferences focusing on just one rotation. Topics and relevant materials for each rotation may include one or more of the following:

Whole- and Small-Group Learning	Independent Reading	Student Application	*Reading Inventory* Results
• Student *ReaL Book* and accompanying *ReaL Book* rubrics and logs • *READ 180* Workshop Assessment reports; Student Test Printout	• Daily reading logs • QuickWrites • Graphic Organizers • Independent Reading Report	• Student Application Report • Writing Zone/Writing Prompt essays • Fluency Check recording	• Lexile Proficiency and Growth Report

Data Analytics & Communication

How to Conference With Students (continued)

What to Review at a Student Conference

Focus each conference on specific elements of student performance. Use current student results and benchmark data to help students understand their progress and articulate their goals for success. Conference on the same aspect of the classroom with all students or tailor the conferences to focus on the area where each student struggles most.

Whole- and Small-Group Learning	Independent Reading	Student Application	Reading Inventory Results
• Participation in daily instruction • Observe Report • Completion and accuracy of *ReaL Book* work • Translation of strategies to Workshop Assessments	• Book selection • Participation and amount read • Independent Reading Report (*Reading Counts!* quiz success)	• Daily participation • Student App results: comprehension, vocabulary, spelling, fluency, and writing results • Student App usage	• Current Lexile level • Expected gain • Grade-level proficiency range

Review *ReaL Book* student Workshop Logs during conferences.

Sharing Results With Families

Sharing progress data with students fosters student buy-in and increases motivation. Use *READ 180*'s assessments and student reports to schedule regular conferences with students. Update them on their progress, help them set goals, and celebrate achievement.

Introducing Your Classroom

Use an Open House or Back-to-School Night to introduce your classroom to families and establish a communication structure so that caregivers feel comfortable contacting you with questions or concerns.

During a classroom introduction, structure time to mirror the Instructional Model process students follow each day, allowing parents and caregivers to spend a little time in each rotational area.

- Use the Blended Learning Model poster to explain each of the rotations.
- Allow parents to read a paperback or listen to an audiobook during Independent Reading.
- Share current student *ReaL Book* work and distribute Parent Letters.
- Offer an opportunity to have follow-up conversations on how to best meet student needs during the course of the school year and establish a structure for regular communication.
- Allow families to share additional information about their child's needs in a survey or during a one-on-one conversation with you.
- Share information about the Family Portal, where caregivers can go to learn more about the program, access research and results, view bilingual videos and tips, and download resources and activities to assist students at home.

Collaborating With Families

Families are a critical link in each student's reading progress. Maintain contact with families throughout the year, sharing achievements and concerns with parents as they happen.

- Send home letters introducing the program and providing classroom updates to the family.
- Schedule conferences to discuss any concerns about student progress.
- Invite families to visit the classroom during the year to read with students in the Independent Reading rotation. If parents have a connection to the current *ReaL Book* Workshop topic, invite them to participate as a guest speaker.

What to Prepare for a Parent-Teacher Conference

Throughout the year, you may wish to hold conferences to speak with families one-on-one regarding their child's performance. Consider the focus of your conference as you gather relevant information. During some conferences you may wish to complete a review of progress in each rotation, while at other times you may wish to have shorter conferences focusing on just one aspect of student performance. Topics and relevant materials for each rotation may include one or more of the following:

Whole- and Small-Group Learning	Independent Reading	Student Application	*Reading Inventory* Results
• Student Portfolio • Student *ReaL Book* and accompanying *ReaL Book* rubrics • *READ 180* Workshop Assessment Report; Student Test Printout	• Daily reading logs • QuickWrites • Graphic Organizers • Independent Reading Report	• *READ 180* Student App Report	• Lexile Proficiency and Growth Report

How to Structure a Parent-Teacher Conference

Focus each conference on specific elements of student performance. Use current student results and benchmark data to help families understand their child's progress and ways they can help facilitate that progress.

1. Understand the conference goals prior to sitting down with families. *What do you hope to communicate and what can families do to help their child at home? What questions or concerns might families have regarding their child's performance?*

2. Gather relevant information. Determine which reports or student work best demonstrate the topics you wish to discuss with parents. Compile these items, remembering not to overwhelm families with too much information.

3. If the families requested the conference, begin the meeting by allowing the family to describe their questions and concerns while you listen. Repeat their concerns back to them to make sure you understood them clearly. Then address concerns one at a time.

4. When you begin sharing information about the student, begin by discussing the positive aspects of the student's performance. Be careful to share specific examples while avoiding using educational jargon without fully explaining the terms (e.g., *Reading Inventory*, rotations, *ReaL Book*, etc.).

5. Work with family to craft a plan to support the student. Set goals and clearly communicate how caregivers can be involved in assisting the student with achieving those goals.

6. End the conference on a positive note, and communicate how and when the family will receive updates.

Additional Resources

Use Resources on HMH Teacher Space to access thousands of point-of-use searchable resources, including materials for differentiation, extra practice, assessment, and professional learning.

Accessing Resources from Teacher Central

Search Options

1. **Collections:** When you first access the Resources tab, you will find resources organized into Collections. Browse through Collection topics such as Implementation Support, Tech Support, Professional Learning, The Student App, and more.

2. **Search and Browse:** Enter a resource name or keyword in the "Search all Resources" field at the top right of the screen. Then click the magnifying glass to view and select resources. Use the filters on the left to narrow down options.

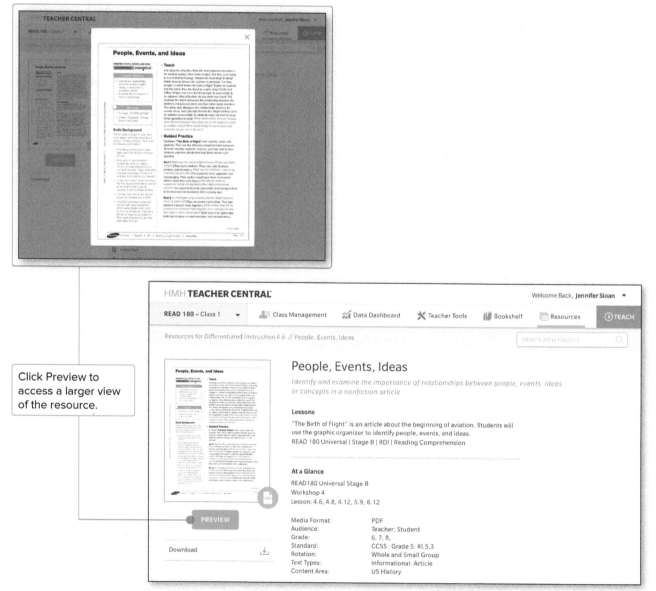

Click Preview to access a larger view of the resource.

HMH Teacher Central: Resources

Resources for Differentiated Instruction

Reading Comprehension

Resources for Differentiated Instruction (RDI) is a set of downloadable resources designed to differentiate instruction by providing extra practice or lessons for skills below, on, and above grade level. Reading Comprehension lessons generally include three components: Instruction, Passage(s), and a Graphic Organizer. The teacher bundle includes an annotated graphic organizer. The passages range in text type and complexity to provide reinforcement for all students.

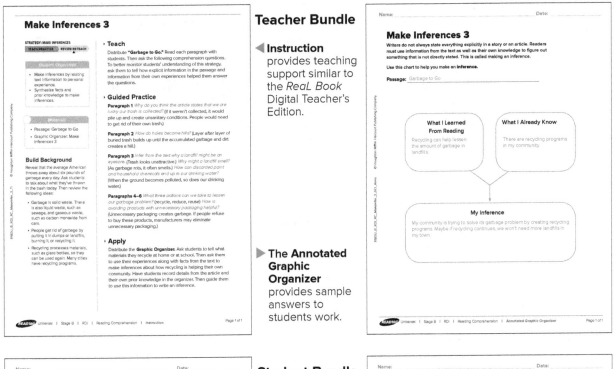

Teacher Bundle

◀ **Instruction** provides teaching support similar to the *ReaL Book* Digital Teacher's Edition.

▶ The **Annotated Graphic Organizer** provides sample answers to students work.

Student Bundle

◀ **Passage(s)** offer a variety of text types written at varying Lexile ranges, designed to support or challenge students as needed. Some lessons include Extend passage(s) that are optional.

▶ The **Graphic Organizer** provides practice for students. Most are also available as independent resources and can be used with other texts.

Independent Reading Resources

The *READ 180* Independent Reading Bookshelf contains a collection of high interest paperbacks, audiobooks, eBooks, and eReads at a variety of levels and genres to provide every student with appropriate texts. Each text has an aligned QuickWrite and Graphic Organizer to aid students in reading comprehension and writing. The teacher bundle includes an annotated graphic organizer.

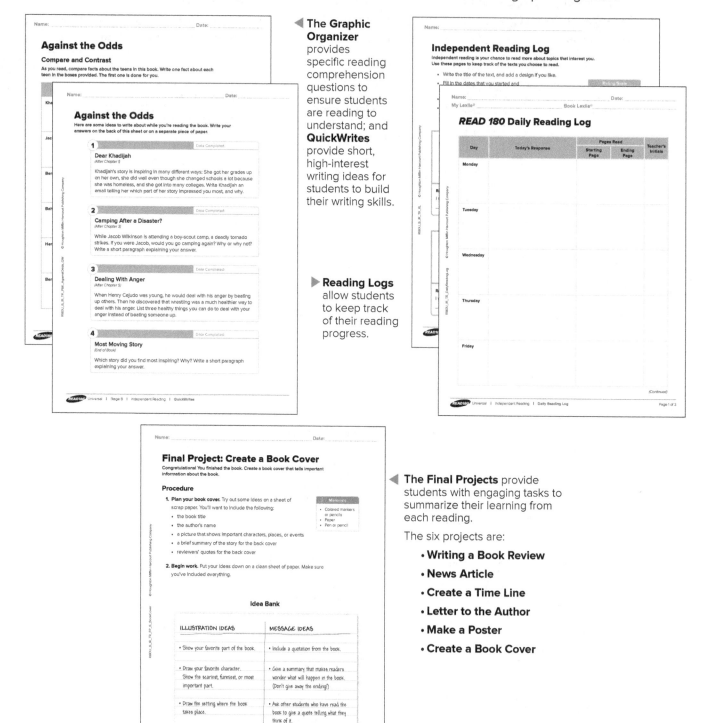

The Graphic Organizer provides specific reading comprehension questions to ensure students are reading to understand; and **QuickWrites** provide short, high-interest writing ideas for students to build their writing skills.

Reading Logs allow students to keep track of their reading progress.

The Final Projects provide students with engaging tasks to summarize their learning from each reading.

The six projects are:

- **Writing a Book Review**
- **News Article**
- **Create a Time Line**
- **Letter to the Author**
- **Make a Poster**
- **Create a Book Cover**

Student Application Resources

All *READ 180* Student Application Segment Overviews, Anchor Texts, and Writing Prompts are available as downloadable resources.

Segment 19: Road to Hope

Anchor Video Summary

Peter Dut had to flee his beautiful village in Sudan during a brutal civil war. Without his parents, and in fear for his life, Peter, along with 20,000 other "Lost Boys," walked hundreds of miles to find safety in a refugee camp in Kenya. The boys survived in the camp for nine years, but had little hope of a prosperous future. When Peter and nearly 4,000 others were brought to the United States to begin new lives, their hard work continued. With effort and help from caring people, Peter found a job, graduated high school, and enrolled in college—ready to take on a much brighter future.

Clusters

This segment appears in the following clusters:
- Freedom Road
- Moving Day
- Uncivil Wars

▸ Power Words

Students are exposed to these high-utility academic and content-area words in the Anchor Video and Anchor Texts, and study them in the Language Zone.

Power Words in the Anchor Video:

All students are introduced to these words in the Anchor Video and study them in the Language Zone. Each Anchor Text includes 4–6 of these words.

Levels 1–6		
adjust	immediately	limited
shelter	succeeded	survive

Additional Power Words in Anchor Texts:

Anchor Texts in Levels 4–6 have up to three additional Power Words. Students encounter these words in the Anchor Texts and study them in the Language Zone.

Level 4	assumed	
Level 5	distribution	settlement
Level 6	circulated	devices	unite

▸ Oral Fluency Practice Benchmarks

Use the benchmarks below to score students' final recordings in the Success Zone. These benchmarks indicate students' level of oral reading fluency with text at their independent reading level.

	Below Benchmark	Approaching Benchmark	On Benchmark
Level 1	110 sec (79 WCPM)	87 sec (100 WCPM)	74 sec (117 WCPM)
Level 2	107 sec (99 WCPM)	89 sec (120 WCPM)	78 sec (137 WCPM)
Level 3	106 sec (109 WCPM)	89 sec (130 WCPM)	80 sec (145 WCPM)
Level 4	114 sec (119 WCPM)	98 sec (139 WCPM)	90 sec (152 WCPM)
Level 5	122 sec (146 WCPM)	110 sec (162 WCPM)	103 sec (173 WCPM)
Level 6	130 sec (161 WCPM)	121 sec (173 WCPM)	119 sec (177 WCPM)

(Continued)

READ180 Universal | Student Application | Segment B.19 | **Segment Overview**   Page 1 of 2

▲ **Segment Overviews** provide at-a-glance information including a summary of the Anchor Video, Power Word vocabulary in the videos and texts by level, Oral Fluency benchmarks for each level, and the comprehension strategies and writing types included in each Segment.

Name: _____   Date: _____

Bionic Man

Hugh Herr started climbing rocks when he was seven years old. As a teenager, he was one of the world's best rock climbers. Then, at age 17, he was caught in a blizzard. Trapped in chest-deep snow for four days, Herr developed severe frostbite. Doctors had to amputate both of his legs below the knee. [13] [27] [40] [51] [55]

Herr learned to walk and climb with artificial limbs, but his new legs couldn't handle rock and ice effectively. So Herr rebuilt his prosthetics, incorporating high-tech climbing tools, and soon, he was climbing better than ever. His custom-made legs gave Herr a new goal: to design superior artificial limbs for other people. [65] [79] [88] [101] [107]

Herr went back to school to study mechanical engineering. Today, he works with a team of scientists who study bionics. They build machines that mimic the function of biological body parts. [117] [129] [148]

One of Herr's most successful inventions is a bionic ankle. To design it, he studied the way biological legs move when people walk, run, and jump. Then he created a bionic ankle with sensors and motors that activate each part at just the right time. Patients can walk, run, and even play soccer. [159] [161] [175] [188] [191]

Herr and his team aren't the only scientists studying bionics, of course. Some scientists are using their knowledge to build bionic exoskeletons. These motorized skeletons are worn over the body, and can even help paralyzed patients walk. ■ [202] [212] [222] [228]

Use for fluency practice.

READ180 Universal | Student Application | Reading Zone | Segment B.5 | Level 4 | Anchor Text   Page 1 of 1

▲ **Anchor Texts** are provided for each Segment at multiple levels to individualize instruction for every student.

Name: _____   Date: _____

Road to Hope

Now that you have finished the segment, write an essay in response to the prompts below. If you've already answered one of the prompts in the Writing Zone, select a different prompt from the options below.

TIDE
- Thesis Statement
- Idea
- Details
- Ending

Informative Writing Prompt

Provide up to three ideas that support your essay. Write at least two details to support each idea.

> **Prompt**
> Explain some of the hardships Peter Dut overcame to live in the United States.

Thesis Statement _____

Ideas _____

Details _____

Ending _____

READ180 Universal | Student Application | Writing Zone | Segment B.19 | Writing Prompt   Page 1 of 2

◀ Each Segment includes two **Writing Prompts** of two different writing types with a writing strategy and outline for support.

READ 180 Workshop Assessment Resources

The *READ 180* Workshop Assessments assess students' transfer of specific reading skills taught in each *ReaL Book* Workshop. They are available in printable and digital formats.

There are two types of Workshop Assessments: **Interim** and **End of Workshop**. The Level a tests are written at a lower level of complexity than the Level b tests.

Name: _____ Data: _____

READ180° Workshop 1 Interim Assessment (Level b)

DIRECTIONS: This is a reading test. Follow the directions for each part of the test, and choose the best answer to each question.

PRACTICE QUESTION A

Read the sentences. Then answer the question that follows.

The hurricane caused a lot of damage to our area. There are plans to <u>rebuild</u> factories that have been destroyed.

What is the meaning of <u>rebuild</u>?

A to make something slowly

B to make again

C to make before

D to make something safe

PRACTICE QUESTION B

Read the paragraph. Then answer the question that follows.

Child labor laws are important. These are laws that support the rights of children. Without these labor laws, young children could be put in dangerous situations. One law that protects the rights of children is the Fair Labor Standards Act. This act sets working age restrictions for children. It also protects children from working conditions that may be unhealthy or unfair.

Based on information in the paragraph, what are **two** goals of child labor laws?

A These laws keep employers from hiring young children.

B These laws create more jobs for children.

C These laws help keep children safe.

D These laws encourage children to learn certain skills.

E These laws help children find jobs in certain areas.

Go on ▶

READ180 Universal I Stage B I ReaL Book I Workshop 1 I Interim Assessment I Level b   Page 1 of 8

Name: _____ Data: _____

READ180° Workshop 1 End-of-Workshop Assessment (Level a)

DIRECTIONS: This is a reading test. Follow the directions for each part of the test, and choose the best answer to each question.

PRACTICE QUESTION A

Read the sentence. Then answer the question that follows.

Employees who have strong skills earn a higher <u>wage</u> than those with no experience.

What does the word <u>wage</u> mean?

A a payment

B a fine

C a gift

D a talent

PRACTICE QUESTION B

Read the paragraph. Then answer the question that follows.

The United Nations (UN) is an important organization. The UN was created in 1945. One of the organization's main goals is to encourage and enforce international peace. It also works to solve problems in countries all over the world. If human rights are not being respected, it helps people work for justice. The UN has offices in different countries. Its main headquarters is in New York City.

Which **two** details support the central idea that the United Nations is an important organization?

A It began in 1945.

B It promotes peace.

C It supports human rights.

D It has more than one office.

E It has headquarters in New York City.

Go on ▶

READ180 Universal I Stage B I ReaL Book I Workshop 1 I End of Workshop I Level a   Page 1 of 15

▲ Administer the **Interim Assessment** at the end of Part 1 of each *ReaL Book* Workshop.

Reading (Comprehension and Vocabulary) *(Continued)*

7. The passage and time line provide information about the assassination of President Kennedy.

Draw a line from each piece of information in the left column to the source of the information in the right column.

Police captured Lee Harvey Oswald the same afternoon that President Kennedy was shot.	Passage
Lee Harvey Oswald worked at the School Book Depository in Dallas.	Time Line
Lee Harvey Oswald's shot also hit Governor Connally.	Passage and Time Line
Lee Harvey Oswald was shot and killed by Jack Ruby.	

8. What conclusion about Lee Harvey Oswald can be drawn from the information in the passage and the time line?

A He had a long history of violence.

B He intended to kill Governor Connally, not President Kennedy.

C He had made threats on other leaders.

D He was arrested but never went to prison for President Kennedy's murder.

Go on ▶

READ180 Universal I Stage B I ReaL Book I Workshop 4 I End of Workshop I Level b   Page 6 of 15

▲ Administer the **End-of-Workshop Assessment** at the end of Part 2.

◀ **The tests** include an array of item types that give students essential practice for the Next Generation Assessments.

Download the **Workshop Assessments Introduction** from the Resources tab on **HMH Teacher Central**.

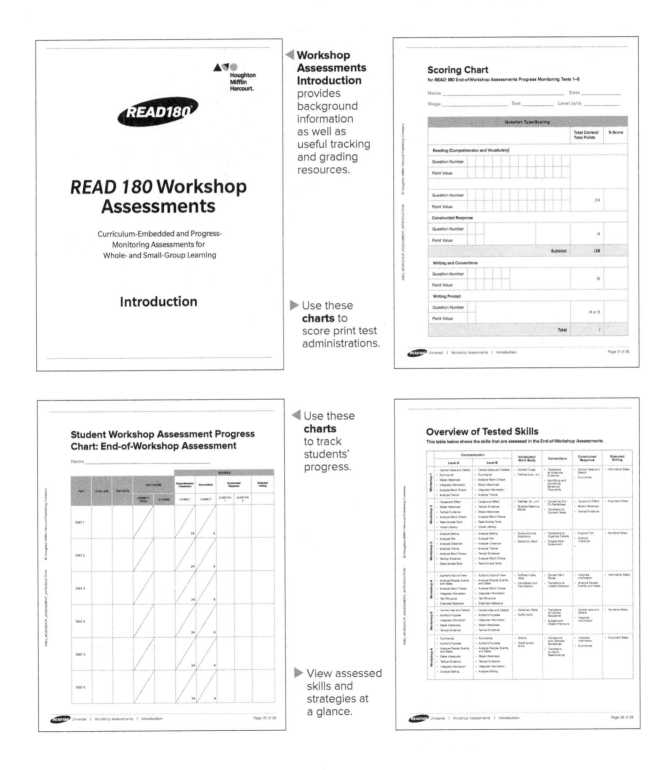

◀ **Workshop Assessments Introduction** provides background information as well as useful tracking and grading resources.

▶ Use these **charts** to score print test administrations.

◀ Use these **charts** to track students' progress.

▶ View assessed skills and strategies at a glance.

Writing Rubrics

READ 180 includes a rubric for each writing type with both a 4- and 6- point scale and scoring sheet. Each rubric is available both as an individual resource and bundled with applicable lessons. They can be used to assess writing in the Student App, Resources for Differentiated Instruction, Workshop Assessments, and *ReaL Book* writing activities.

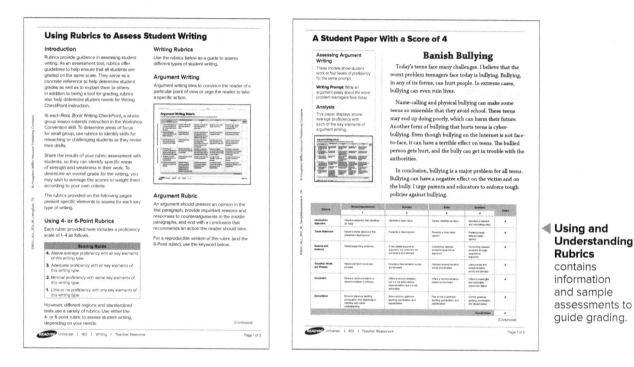

◀ **Using and Understanding Rubrics** contains information and sample assessments to guide grading.

◀ There are **rubrics** for the following writing types:

- **Opinion**
- **Argument**
- **Narrative**
- **Informative**
- **Informational Summary**
- **Literary Analysis**
- **Research Paper**

My Progress Charts

Download these tracking charts to build student motivation. During student conferences be sure to review these logs and highlight streaks and successes.

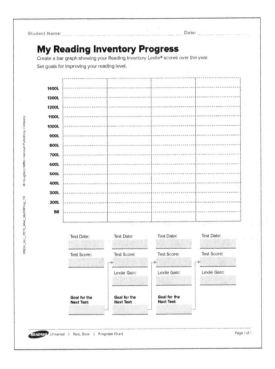

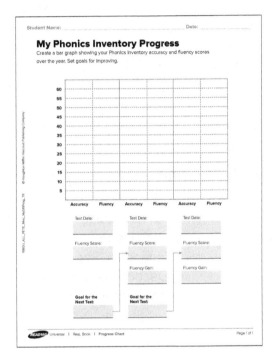

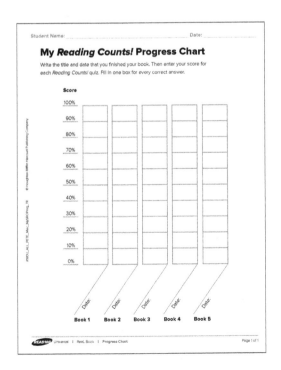

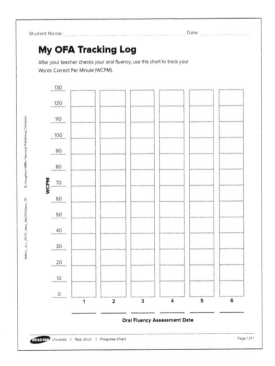

Appendix 1

Notes Regarding Use of HMH *Reading Inventory* as a Progress Monitor for *System 44* Students

What is the appropriate assessment to measure growth for *System 44* students?

HMH *Phonics Inventory* is the appropriate assessment to measure growth for *System 44* students. The *Phonics Inventory* is a screener and progress monitor that measures foundational reading skills, including the accuracy and fluency with which students identify individual letters and words and decode nonwords. HMH *Reading Inventory* is a screener and progress monitor that measures reading comprehension, a skill that requires sufficient fluency with foundational skills. Since students in *System 44* and similar Tier 3 interventions are still developing foundational skills, their growth is more accurately measured with *Phonics Inventory*. Only once students are Advancing Decoders is *Reading Inventory* an appropriate measure of their reading growth.

Should *Reading Inventory* growth expectations be used for *System 44* students?

While it is possible for students in *System 44* or similar Tier 3 interventions to demonstrate growth on *Reading Inventory*, *Reading Inventory* growth expectations should only be used once students are Advancing Decoders, indicating that they are decoding text with sufficient fluency to support comprehension. For students with a *Phonics Inventory* decoding status of Pre-Decoder, Beginning Decoder, or Developing Decoder, *Phonics Inventory* fluency scores should be used as an indicator of their growth towards comprehension.

Appendix 2

HMH recommends administering *The Reading Inventory* close to the beginning of the school year for initial placement purposes. HMH recognizes that school districts begin the school year at different time points on the calendar. In the chart below, fall refers to the time period between July 15–November 30 of the current school year. The placement recommendations for fall are derived from the spring *Reading Inventory* Reading Comprehension Assessment Performance Bands using the student's prior grade level at the time of fall testing.

Fall Placement Recommendations (Current School Year)			
Current Grade	Eligible for Tier 2/*Read 180* or Tier 3/*System 44*	Eligible for *Read 180*	Eligible for Tier 1
4	BR to 400L	405 to 515L	520L and Above
5	BR to 400L	405 to 735L	740L and Above
6	BR to 600L	605 to 825L	830L and Above
7	BR to 600L	605 to 920L	925L and Above
8	BR to 600L	605 to 965L	970L and Above
9	BR to 600L	605 to 1005L	1010L and Above
10	BR to 600L	605 to 1045L	1050L and Above
11 and 12	BR to 600L	605 to 1075L	1080L and Above
Recommendation	Administer *Phonics Inventory* to determine if *READ 180*/Tier 2 or *System 44*/Tier 3 is more appropriate.	Enroll in *READ 180* or Tier 2 Intervention.	Enroll in Core program.

*Fall is from July 15–November 30 of current school year. Grade level corresponds to grade level at time of testing within fall window.

Appendix 3

While HMH recommends administering *The Reading Inventory* close to the beginning of the school year for initial placement purposes, HMH recognizes the need for placement recommendations for students who may need to be placed into an intervention outside of the fall (July 15–November 30) window. In the chart below, spring refers to the time period between April 1 and July 14 of the current school year. The placement recommendations for spring are derived from the spring *Reading Inventory* Reading Comprehension Assessment Performance Bands using the student's current grade level at the time of spring testing. For students who take their initial *Reading Inventory* outside of the fall or spring time periods, educators should use their best judgment as to which placement recommendations to follow.

Spring Placement Recommendations (Current School Year)			
Current Grade	Eligible for Tier 2/*Read 180* or Tier 3/*System 44*	Eligible for *Read 180*	Eligible for Tier 1
4	BR to 400L	405 to 735L	740L and Above
5	BR to 400L	405 to 825L	830L and Above
6	BR to 600L	605 to 920L	925L and Above
7	BR to 600L	605 to 965L	970L and Above
8	BR to 600L	605 to 1005L	1010L and Above
9	BR to 600L	605 to 1045L	1050L and Above
10	BR to 600L	605 to 1075L	1080L and Above
11 and 12	BR to 600L	605 to 1180L	1185L and Above
Recommendation	Administer *Phonics Inventory* to determine if *READ 180*/Tier 2 or *System 44*/Tier 3 is more appropriate.	Enroll in *READ 180* or Tier 2 Intervention.	Enroll in Core program.

*Spring is from April 1–July 14 of the current school year. Grade level corresponds to grade level at time of testing within spring window.

Appendix 4

Based on a student's spring Lexile score, HMH recommends that students who are Proficient and Advanced on the spring *Reading Inventory* Reading Comprehension Assessment Performance Bands are eligible for Tier 1 or Core instruction. The chart below outlines the Lexile levels corresponding to each *READ 180* grade level 4–12.

Spring Exit Recommendations (Current School Year)	
Current Grade	**Eligible for Tier 1**
4	740L and Above
5	830L and Above
6	925L and Above
7	970L and Above
8	1010L and Above
9	1050L and Above
10	1080L and Above
11 and 12	1185L and Above
Recommendation	Enroll in Core program.

Appendix 5

The HMH *Reading Inventory* Spring Reading Comprehension Assessment Performance Bands reflect the grade-level expectations of college and career readiness standards for spring of the current year during which testing occurred.

Reading Comprehension Assessment Performance Bands				
Grade	Below Basic	Basic	Proficient	Advanced
K	N/A	BR	0L to 275L	280L and Above
1	BR	0L to 185L	190L to 530L	535L and Above
2	BR to 215L	220L to 415L	420L to 650L	655L and Above
3	BR to 325L	330L to 515L	520L to 820L	825L and Above
4	BR to 535L	540L to 735L	740L to 940L	945L and Above
5	BR to 615L	620L to 825L	830L to 1010L	1015L and Above
6	BR to 725L	730L to 920L	925L to 1070L	1075L and Above
7	BR to 765L	770L to 965L	970L to 1120L	1125L and Above
8	BR to 785L	790L to 1005L	1010L to 1185L	1190L and Above
9	BR to 845L	850L to 1045L	1050L to 1260L	1265L and Above
10	BR to 885L	890L to 1075L	1080L to 1335L	1340L and Above
11/12	BR to 980L	985L to 1180L	1185L to 1385L	1390L and Above